THE COMPLETE
BREAD MACHINE
COOKBOOK

THE COMPLETE
BREAD MACHINE
COOKBOOK

Over 100 classic and contemporary recipes, techniques and tips for every kind of machine

EBURY PRESS
LONDON

To my loyal husband and dearest friend, who has worked with me non-stop for the past year and a half on this book, acting as my chauffeur, shopper, washer-upper, note-taker, scientific advisor and general assistant.

First published in 2001

5 7 9 10 8 6 4

Text and recipe copyright © Sonia Allison 2001
Photography copyright © Ebury Press 2001

First published by Ebury Press
Random House, 20 Vauxhall Bridge Road, London SW1V 2SA

Random House Australia (Pty) Limited
20 Alfred Street, Milsons Point, Sydney, New South Wales 2061, Australia

Random House New Zealand Limited
18 Poland Road, Glenfield, Auckland 10, New Zealand

Random House South Africa (Pty) Limited
Endulini, 5A Jubilee Road, Parktown 2193, South Africa

The Random House Group Limited Reg. No. 954009

www.randomhouse.co.uk

A CIP catalogue record for this book is available from the British Library

ISBN 0 09 187957 4

Editor: Amanda Howard
Designer: Christine Wood
Photographer: Craig Robertson
Home Economist: Sonia Allison
Food Stylist: Julie Beresford
Stylist: Helen Trent

Colour separation by Colorlito, Milan
Printed and bound in Singapore by Tien Wah Press

Contents

introduction

Bread is an emotive, wholesome and nourishing food staple that has sustained and comforted mankind, rich and poor, throughout its long history.

The whole process of wheat milling began as early as 6500BC when the enterprising and industrious Ancient Egyptians ground locally grown wheat grains between heavy stones to produce a coarse and rugged brownish meal. Cooked long and slowly with water, the softened meal turned into a gruel or porridge-like mush and became a plain but important feature in the diet of the time. The next step appears to have been the transition to what are now commonly referred to as bannocks — unleavened flat cakes made from semi-crushed grains moistened with water and left to dry over heat or, more conveniently, outdoors in the hot Egyptian sun. The cakes were hard and dry, not unlike modern day crispbreads, and sustained the population for a further 2,000 years.

The progression from flat to leavened bread is attributed to both the ancient Egyptians and Hebrews and probably came about by accident, around 4000BC, when a dough made from water and meal, left forgotten for a day or so, attracted natural yeasts from the atmosphere and started to swell and ferment in the warmth. It was probably the origin of sour dough, a leaven in itself, and one of the earliest known natural raising agents.

The cultivation of various wheats continued to flourish and thrive under the Egyptians but it was finally the Romans who mastered the art of milling by inventing the millstone, the rotary quern, which resembled a pestle and mortar made from heavy stone and which was the forerunner of the millstones used today for, appropriately enough, stoneground flour. And it was the Romans who brought bread to Britain.

Looking back on my own personal history, I recall my family were much more involved with cooking than they were with baking. Bread, cakes and biscuits were always shop-bought so there was no incentive for me to bake anything, leave alone bread which I always considered a professional baker's craft. Even my student days did little to encourage me, despite keen and conscientious teaching.

Years later, student and teaching days long gone, my interest in breadmaking, or yeast cookery as it was once known, was rekindled when I worked closely with an organisation whose job it was to promote flour. My colleagues were scientists with impressive degrees, adept at explaining the ins and outs of breadmaking and all its ramifications. I, in turn, had an expert and well-experienced team of home economists from Britain and Australia working with me. Between us all we covered literally every aspect of baking and in later life it has become an on-going hobby that I cherish.

Preventing me from baking as I used to in the old days is that ever-present scenario called modern life, an all-too-familiar challenging state of affairs where leisure is a precious commodity and short-cuts are in order and gladly accepted by some of our distinguished and more serious-minded food gurus and writers – just watch the TV cooks. Few look down on the time-saving food mixer used in the kitchens of the humble and the mighty. And what about blenders and the do-it-all Magimix, ice cream makers, juice extractors, citrus squeezers, sandwich makers, potato peelers, microwaves, and now bread machines? We have moved into an automated, labour-saving world, giving home cooks of all persuasions their very own Jeeves at affordable prices.

When breadmakers first appeared on the scene over here I was sceptical. I remembered those happy and relaxed days of kneading doughs, slapping them about on the table with abandon and venting all my frustrations on a batch of hot cross buns-to-be. Brilliant therapy. Then a recent business visit to New York made me think again. Breadmakers were one of the hottest tickets in town, as they have become over here, moving off the shelves of well-known stores with lightning speed. And books on the subject, from simple paperbacks to colour-packed hardbacks, were thick on the ground in leading bookshops akin to Waterstones and WHSmith. I brought a lightweight paperback home with me but the recipes were geared to North American tastes and measures and needed amending. It was bothersome and time-consuming and at that point I decided to buy a machine, try it out and maybe write my own book more suited to British tastes. I invested in a cheapie from Argos and it worked magnificently without any help from me. I started making loaves on a daily basis –

friends, family, neighbours and the freezer all benefited – and when I was occupied with something else, my husband willingly took over. 'It's SO easy,' he said, and he meant it.

Since those early days just a few months ago, manufacturers have generously loaned me a plethora of machines in every price range and size to try out and, with their help and that of Allinson's Flours, I have worked successfully on family recipes that are delicious, nutritious and additive-free (other than the herbs, spices, sugar and flavourings or dried fruits and nuts you add yourself). I have also focused on breads, buns and cakes from around the world in addition to catering for minority groups with dietary problems like those unable to tolerate dairy foods and fats, and others with coeliac disease who are sensitive to wheat and need to follow a gluten-free diet.

If you stop and think about it for a moment, you'll agree nothing warms the heart and cheers the soul quite as much as the smell of freshly baked bread wafting out of the kitchen and nothing shop bought, however expensive, can ever match the luxurious taste and texture of a high-rise and golden-crusted loaf you've made yourself. My hope now is that your enthusiasm and curiosity have been tweaked and you'll want to share something of my passion for the ancient craft of modern baking, the easy way, with a breadmaker for guaranteed success.

Sonia Allison

about breadmakers

A gimmick? Another worktop 'thing' destined for the back of a cupboard? A waste of money? Hardly. In the USA breadmakers continue to sweep through the country like a forest fire, turning even the most elementary, inexperienced and cautious cooks – men as well as women – into a nation of enthusiastic and dedicated bakers. Over here, they are the new kids on the block, a little late coming (about 1997) but now settling down contentedly throughout Britain and transforming baking habits more rapidly than anyone ever anticipated, least of all the flour merchants and the machine manufacturers themselves. Essentially compact electrical units, breadmakers give you your own personal bakehouse which, provided you heed the rules to the letter, produce stylish and fine-tasting loaves over and over and over again at approximately 7p to 8p a go plus the cost of ingredients. It's a bit of a waste of time comparing shop-bought prices with homemade: the DIY breadmaker bread sometimes works out dearer than supermarket loaves but look what you're getting – top-quality ingredients of your own choice matched by magnificent, well-formed and shapely loaves with a taste of heaven and a smell of yesteryear for anyone who still remembers what the food of yesteryear was like, or wants to find out. Who could ask for more?

Although most breadmakers look alike, each model has its own idiosyncrasies, its own personality and its own behavioural problems. These you learn by experience and practice so if you have one or two failures to begin with, keep going because you'll win in the end. The first thing to do when you've brought the breadmaker home is sit down in a quiet corner and study the manual and recipes provided by the manufacturer. This will tell you in detail how the machine works, how you fit the paddle into the bucket and then the bucket itself into the breadmaker, and will explain what each setting means – some breadmakers have as many as eleven or even more – and also advise you on how to use the delayed timer for an overnight bake so that you wake up to fresh bread for breakfast. The essential thing to remember with this programme is not to add perishables like milk or eggs that may deteriorate while waiting to be mixed in the middle of the night or early morning.

As far as breadmaking and yeast cookery are concerned, forget everything you ever learned in the past. The techniques in a bread maker are totally different. YOU have nothing to do other than load the ingredients into the non-stick bucket (fitted with its non-stick paddle) in the order given, fix it into the metal-lined breadmaker, close the lid, set the programme you want, press the start button and go away and do something else while the machine works through its programme. No skill required but a few words of caution first.

◆ Make sure the breadmaker is located in a dry and draught-free room at a comfortable room temperature, neither too hot nor too cold. NEVER use it outdoors, in a garage, in the direct heat of hot sun or near a hob or oven. Also make sure the machine has space around itself as it may overheat if confined, which could damage it and/or spoil the bread.

◆ Almost all breadmakers come with an opaque plastic measuring cup of 225 ml/8 fl oz, which equates to the US standard cup measure used by North Americans instead of scales. Also provided is a plastic stalk with a 15 ml/1 tbsp measure at one end and a 5 ml/1 tsp measure at the other. If you prefer to use weights and measures (as I do) rather than cups for greater accuracy, there are handy metric and imperial conversion charts on pages 168–69 which also take cup measures into account.

◆ When the breadmaker bucket is being fed with ingredients, it is ESSENTIAL to avoid contact between the liquid, the sensitive yeast and the salt. Liquid will activate the yeast and make it work too soon, while salt might kill it off altogether. My technique, and no other book tells you this, is to put the liquids into the bucket, add half the flour only and then sprinkle it with additives like salt, sugar and dried milk (if used) in any order. Finally I add the remaining flour in a semi dome, make a small indent in the centre with the back of a teaspoon and pour in the yeast. It has never failed me yet and I've worked with twelve different breadmakers for this book, in every price range from £50 to £200, and experimented with hundreds of loaves. (See my note on the Panasonic machine on page 11).

◆ Although you are advised not to peep and keep opening and shutting the lid (except when using the Panasonic), it's a good idea to look inside while the dough is being kneaded – but NEVER while it's rising and baking – and spatula in any loose flour. This will prevent areas of unmixed flour settling on the outside of the bread and spoiling its appearance. I am not too happy about adding 15 ml/1 tbsp or so of water if the dough looks too dry or doing the same with extra flour if it looks too wet. Some books say you should but I've never had much success doing this.

◆ If there is an irritant with any breadmaker then it has to be the paddle. It has a habit of settling itself cosily inside the base of the loaf and staying there. If you yank it out while the bread is hot you'll tear the crust and burn your fingers quite fiercely, so leave well alone until the bread is cold and gently ease out the paddle; it makes less of a tear. My husband, a sudden and completely unexpected breadmaking freak, uses small pliers padded with a bit of cloth – to prevent damaging the non-stick coating – or strong tweezers. Either implement makes good sense when you think about it. The Team Machine people provide a long hook for their own twin-paddled breadmaker that gets inside the paddles, enabling them to be to eased out. If the paddle should stay in the base of the bucket, as it does sometimes, you may have a job removing it. Pliers again can come in useful. However, if you brush the spindle on which the paddle sits with light oil, and brush the inside of the paddle with more oil using a slender bottle brush BEFORE EVERY BAKE, it encourages the paddle to come out more readily. It's worth a try. If the paddle refuses to shift at all costs, leave the bucket with the paddle stuck in place to soak for a while in hot soapy water. Once removed, rinse the paddle and bucket thoroughly and wipe dry.

◆ While a breadmaker is kneading the dough, you will hear periodic light thumping noises as the dough is pushed from one side of the bucket to the other. The noise is no worse than the drone of a vacuum cleaner or a washing machine going through its paces. Though some complain, it's bearable because the action is relatively short-lived.

◆ Before plunging headlong into the recipes in my book, make up the basic ones given in your breadmaker manual first. This will give you an idea of what to expect from your own breadmaker and also give you the confidence to be more adventurous.

◆ If you come up against snags and you consider your bread a disappointment, be guided by the Faults and Reasons section on page 165–67.

◆ Although most of the machines I tested have a cakes and jam programme, I have concentrated on bread and dough only. If you want to experiment, be guided by the instruction manual.

hints

If using the larger machines with twin paddles, such as the models made by Team International and Prima, you can make up any of the recipes in this book, using 1½ times the amounts given. If the mix is plain without additions, you can even double the quantities.

using the Panasonic machine

This machine is one of the few that tells you to add the yeast first, followed by dry ingredients followed by liquids. To make successful loaves and doughs in the Panasonic using my recipes, all you have to do is reverse the order in which the ingredients are added to the bucket, using the breadmaker instruction book supplied as a guide.

danger!

Don't touch the outside of any machine during the baking cycle as it sometimes gets quite hot and can cause burns.

slicing the loaf

Lie the bread on its side and cut downwards for conventional-looking slices. For long slices, cut from top to bottom.

a last word

Like human beings, no two loaves look exactly the same, some being more handsome and better-shaped than others. Quirks like a lopsided top crust or slight bumps or dips do occur from time to time but usually have minimal effect on the quality of the bread. Beauty is only crust deep.

breadmaking ingredients

wheat

Used worldwide, wheat is an ancient and versatile grain, a long-established and trusted staple for commercial and domestic baking and, to a lesser extent, cooking. The main type used for milling is known as common wheat (*Triticum aestivum*) but within this species are to be found other variants, developed and modified over centuries of cultivation. A wheat grain is made up of three specific parts, namely the germ, endosperm and finally a protective covering or overcoat of bran. The germ is the embryo of the grain and, given the opportunity and right conditions, will grow into a new wheat plant. The germ can be found in wheatmeal flour and may also be added to other flours (not less than 10 per cent) to make wheatgerm flour. The endosperm, or heart of the grain, comprises the aleurone layer that is rich in proteins and vitamins while the endosperm itself is high in starch (over 80 per cent) and is the basis of white flour. In breadmaking, starch plays an important role; the process of fermentation converts it to sugars that, in turn, feed and activate the yeast. The bran consists of the outer, protective layers of the grain and is added, in varying amounts, to wholemeal and brown flour. The wheat grain, in its raw state, is indigestible and the outer layers have to be crushed or milled before the grain can be used. Historically, this was done by grinding the wheat between two stones but towards the end of the eighteenth century the roller mill was introduced, a technique whereby the bran and germ are separated from the starch. During the milling process the grain is cleaned, dried and conditioned. It is then passed through rollers that break open and crush the grain and the wheat is subsequently sifted and purified in order to separate the germ and bran. The process of milling and sieving continues until fine white flour is produced. Bran and wheatgerm are streamed into the white flour to make brown or wholemeal flour and at this stage a raising agent (baking powder) can be added to make self-raising flour. Finally the flour is sifted at the mill before packaging. The addition of calcium and iron with niacin and thiamin (the last two being vitamins of the B group) is a legal requirement in all flours. Wholemeal flour already contains these nutrients naturally although it has less calcium.

gluten

Gluten is an essential ingredient for successful breadmaking, a wheat protein with elastic-like properties. When a dough is formed with flour, yeast and liquid and then thoroughly kneaded, strands of gluten are woven into a kind of network or mesh, creating the framework of the bread. As the kneading continues – and the breadmaker does a brilliant job of this – the gluten cells become interwoven, trapping bubbles of carbon dioxide gas (also a raising agent) released by the yeast. The carbon dioxide then expands and raises or 'lifts' the dough. It is therefore extremely important to choose the correct flour with a high protein or gluten content – anything from 10.5 per cent upwards – so read the section on flour below carefully as certain flours, such as organic or those not marked 'strong', will be unsuitable for use in a breadmaker by themselves.

recommended flours

STRONG WHOLEMEAL BREAD FLOUR

The best wholemeal bread flour is milled using a traditional millstone. As with all good wholemeal flours, it should contain the wholewheat grain (100 per cent extraction) that retains all the natural nutrients of the wheat. Nothing is added and nothing taken away. Wholemeal flours are rich in B vitamins and contain considerable amounts of fibre, iron and calcium. However, because the presence of the bran reduces the effectiveness of the gluten during breadmaking, is is important to bear in mind that wholemeal bread dough does not rise as well as white bread dough. As a result, wholemeal bread often has a more dense, moist texture and has less spring to it than white bread. This can be alleviated by using a proportion of white flour – say a third – to the wholemeal.

STRONG WHITE BREAD FLOUR

After the extraction of the bran and germ during the milling process, a white flour of approximately 70–75 per cent extraction is produced. The flour is high in starch with some proteins and B vitamins. It has a very high gluten content which makes it particularly suitable for breadmaking. (See section on gluten, page 12).

COUNTRY GRAIN STRONG BROWN BREAD FLOUR

A strong flour with added malted wheat flakes. These not only add nutritive value to the bread but also give it a nutty taste. This flour is also known as malted wheatgrain or granary.

SOFTGRAIN STRONG WHITE BREAD FLOUR

This is strong white bread flour with the addition of cracked rye and wheat grains. It has a higher fibre (bran) content than ordinary strong white flour and gives bread a more interesting texture and 'bite'.

other flours used in this book

If any of these flours are difficult to find in your local supermarket, try a health food shop or speciality pharmacy.

BARLEY

A low-gluten flour milled from barley, an ancient grain that goes back some 6,000 years and highly esteemed by the ancient Greeks, Romans and Hebrews for breadmaking. A small proportion may be used with strong flours as it contributes a sweet, nutty flavour to the bread and very slightly softens the texture.

BUCKWHEAT

A distinctively flavoured and fairly dark flour, also low in gluten. It cannot be used alone to make bread so is best combined with a strong flour (see Blini Bread, page 28). It lends a rugged, almost musty taste to a sensual and unusual bread.

CORNFLOUR

A very soft flour made from maize. It cannot stand alone in breadmaking as it is gluten-free but a small amount may be added to strong flour to give a more cake-like texture.

CORNMEAL

A semolina look-alike, a small amount of cornmeal (or polenta) adds a splash of colour and a crunchy texture to bread.

GRAM FLOUR

Much used in the Indian sub-continent, gram flour is made from milled chickpeas and is a useful addition to wheat flour when making chapattis and assorted flat breads as it adds an individual taste and texture.

POTATO FLOUR

Potato flour is stark white, gluten-free and fairly flavourless, but small amounts added to wholemeal flour can produce bread that is less dense in structure.

RICE FLOUR

As white as potato flour if made from white rice with the bran and germ removed, this is also starchy and gluten-free and lightens and softens bread if used in small quantities. Brown rice flour, available from health food shops, is a more earthy and tasty option and is healthier in that it contains the bran. Bread made with rice flour has a sweetish, slightly nutty flavour and a fine texture.

RYE FLOUR

Rye was planted by the Romans and it became the staple food crop in the Europe of the Middle Ages where it was mixed with barley to make coarse bread. It flourishes better in a cool climate than a warm one which explains why it is used so extensively for breads and crispbreads in parts of central and northern Europe (Germany in particular), Scandinavia and Russia. Although it has a higher gluten content than some of the flours listed above, it still makes a dense, dark bread and, to suit British tastes, it should be mixed with strong white and wholemeal flours to lighten the texture.

SEMOLINA

A small amount, substituted for some strong flour, gives the bread a slightly grainy texture and an attractive colour.

SOYA FLOUR

A gluten-free flour rich in protein, a small amount combined with strong wheat flour makes bread look creamier and taste moister.

SPELT FLOUR

An ancient form of wheat (*Triticum spelta*) which, when milled into wholemeal flour, contains some gluten and is therefore able to be made by traditional methods into excellent bread with a fine flavour but needs to be mixed with some strong white bread flour to succeed in a breadmaker. The type of gluten found in spelt flour is said to be tolerated by those on a gluten-free diet but a GP should be consulted first.

STORING FLOUR, DOUGH AND BREAD

Flour hates moisture and dampness so must be kept in a cool, dry place and preferably in a lidded, airtight container. Because wholemeal flour has a slightly higher fat content than white, it will not keep as long. Note use by dates carefully. If you want to store flour safely for occasional use, freeze it in airtight containers or in securely tied freezer bags. It is important to bring the flour back to kitchen temperature before using it for bread, especially if yeast is involved. You can freeze prepared dough for up to about five days provided there are no perishable ingredients in the mixture. It must be very securely wrapped first and completely thawed before using, then treated as fresh dough. Loaves of bread or parts of loaves should be put into plastic bags, well-sealed and frozen for three to four weeks.

15

other ingredients

YEAST

Yeast is a living organism and, like many other living things, depends on a ready supply of oxygen, food, moisture and warmth to survive. When dried, however, it will remain dormant until it is activated by liquid. It is used extensively as a leavening agent in the breadmaking process since all the conditions necessary for yeast to grow are present in bread dough; the yeast will cause the carbohydrates (initially sugars) present to ferment and produce carbon dioxide (CO_2). The CO_2 becomes trapped in the dough by the gluten strands and this in turn makes the dough rise and swell and often double or treble in size. Easybake yeast is ideal for breadmakers (see About Breadmakers, pages 8–11) as it is a combination of dried yeast and the bread improver ascorbic acid (vitamin C). Some books recommend adding a little vitamin C powder to a yeast mix but easybake yeasts have it already built in to give a well-balanced and convenient product so no further additives are necessary. The way easybake yeast is formulated means that it is both easy to use and effective. The yeast is first dried before being compressed into thin strands. These break down further into particles that do not need to go through the hydration process before being added to the other ingredients. The vitamin C or ascorbic acid content additionally guarantees the fast action of the yeast by strengthening the protein structure, enabling the dough to trap carbon dioxide and therefore rise more effectively. It is available in 7 g sachets and the best before date is printed on every one. Note that once opened, a sachet must be used immediately as it deteriorates and becomes inactive in a relatively short space of time. To prevent waste, the sachet may be well sealed and refrigerated overnight if you know you are going to be baking again the following day. If not, throw it away.

The little cans or sealed drums of traditional dried active yeast are unsuitable for use in a breadmaker.

SALT

Salt brings out the flavour of bread and also stops the yeast from overworking. However, because it retards the action of the yeast, it should be used

judiciously; 2.5–5ml/½–1 tsp to every 450 g/ 1 lb/3 cups of flour. Do NOT use salt substitutes.

SWEETENERS

The types of sweeteners to use, in the form of sugar, honey, syrup or treacle, have been given in all the recipes where appropriate together with amounts. Please do not vary quantities as the action of the yeast may be retarded and the loaf fall in on itself. Sweeteners are used to improve the flavour and crust colour but, when making bread with dried and crystallised fruits, which are usually sugary, plus additional sweetener, use the sweet setting on your machine if it has one, or set the crust colour to light to prevent the crust darkening too much. On the sweet programme, the bread may be cooked more quickly and/or at a lower temperature. Check with your breadmaker manual for guidance.

WATER

Water is the main liquid used for making bread but there are a number of alternatives – from beetroot or fruit juice to beef consommé and dilute syrups – given where applicable throughout the book. Your own manual will advise what temperature the liquid should be as it can vary from cool to warm, depending on the breadmaker. This MUST be obeyed!

MILK

Milk, when used, is mostly added in dried form – usually skimmed powder or granules for convenience and consistency. It adds nutritional value and also improves crust colour by making it slightly browner. Fresh milk, diluted evaporated milk, yoghurt or buttermilk may be substituted for part of the water. If you decide to use milk only, opt for skimmed or semi-skimmed to prevent the bread from being close-textured.

FATS AND OILS

Melted butter, margarine, lard if you prefer, white cooking fat or any good-quality vegetable oil is acceptable for use in a breadmaker. You will notice extra virgin olive oil has been used only in the Mediterranean style breads only as not everyone likes its pronounced flavour in, say, a breakfast or tea bread. Fats and oils enrich bread and also make it softer and more attractively coloured. Do NOT use low-fat spreads or butter substitutes.

EGGS

Eggs are added for colour, richness and nutritional value. They must be at kitchen temperature and made up to the amount of liquid in the recipe, not used as an extra. You will notice that breads made with eggs have a longer shelf life than those without.

OATS

Low-gluten again, rolled and toasted oats, together with oatmeal, add an interesting texture to white bread. Flour made from oatmeal alone doesn't make satisfactory bread, though small amounts may be used in conjunction with strong flour. It has a high protein content and a pleasant taste.

DRIED FRUITS, NUTS, GRATED CHEESE, HERBS AND SPICES, FLAVOURINGS

Add any of these when your instruction manual tells you. It is usually indicated by a number of bleeps just prior to the end of the second kneading cycle but the most practical piece of advice comes from Morphy Richards: in most cases, the added ingredients are broken apart during the initial kneading cycle so if it is more convenient for you to add them at the start, results will be fine. The paddle is not sharp so additions will remain in reasonable-sized pieces but the final choice has to be yours.

GLAZES FOR BAKED BREADS

Brush glazes over the top crust as soon as the loaf has been removed from its bucket to give the top a gleam and a shimmer.

BEATEN EGG

Brush well-beaten whole egg or lightly beaten white or yolk over the top while the bread is hot. Sprinkle with seeds to taste (for example sesame, caraway or poppy). The eggs sets and 'cooks' on top of the hot bread and holds the seeds in place. If preferred, use toasted dessicated coconut, crushed lump sugar or demerara sugar for sweet breads or seasoning salts and blends for savoury ones.

CORNFLOUR

An old-fashioned glaze but inexpensive and effective. Combine 5 ml/1 tsp of cornflour smoothly with a little cold water. Tip into a small saucepan and add about 60 ml/4 tbsp of hot water. Cook very slowly, stirring, until mixture clears and thickens. Use straight away by applying with a pastry brush.

MILK OR CREAM

Evaporated milk or single cream gives the top crust a pleasing glaze. Brush over with a pastry brush while the bread is still hot.

BUTTER OR MARGARINE

Melt a little butter or margarine in a small dish in the microwave or in a small saucepan over a low heat and brush over the top crust with a pastry brush. It softens the crust and improves the flavour.

JAM, SYRUP, HONEY OR SMOOTH MARMALADE

Use to brush over sweet breads and sticky buns.

GLACÉ ICING

Work a little sifted icing sugar to a fairly thick paste with a small quantity of warm water. Spread over the top of sweet breads, cakes and buns.

traditional breads

BASIC WHITE LOAF

A superbly flavoured classic bread for all occasions, with a golden crust and silken texture.

275 ml/10 fl oz/1¼ cups water

2 tbsp oil

450 g/16 oz/3 cups strong white bread flour

1¼ tsp salt

1½ tsp caster sugar

2 tbsp dried skimmed milk powder or granules

1½ tsp instant or fast-acting dried yeast

glaze to taste (see page 19)

Pour the water into the breadmaker bucket, then add the oil and half the flour. Sprinkle with the salt, sugar and dried milk. Cover with the remaining flour and mound the yeast into the centre. Fit the bucket into the breadmaker and set to the programme recommended in the manual (usually basic white or No 1). When ready, carefully shake the loaf out of the bucket on to a wire cooling rack and stand the right way up. If liked, brush with the selected glaze. Leave the loaf for at least an hour before cutting and/or removing the paddle if necessary.

LARGER SIZE BASIC WHITE LOAF

300 ml/11 fl oz/1⅜ cups water

2 tbsp oil

500 g/17½ oz/3½ cups strong white bread flour

1½ tsp salt

2 tsp caster sugar

2 tbsp dried skimmed milk powder or granules

2 tsp instant or fast-acting dried yeast

glaze to taste (see page 19)

Prepare and bake exactly as for Basic White Loaf.

MALTED WHEAT BREAD

The ultimate brown bread, malty, slightly grainy and with the merest trace of stickiness. It goes well with any sweet or savoury accompaniments.

300 ml/11 fl oz/1⅜ cups water

1 tbsp oil

450 g/16 oz/3 cups country grain strong brown bread flour

2 tsp salt

2 tsp soft brown sugar

1 tbsp dried skimmed milk powder or granules

1½ tsp instant or fast-acting dried yeast

glaze to taste (see page 19)

Pour the water into the breadmaker bucket, then add the oil and half the flour. Sprinkle with the salt, sugar and dried milk. Cover with the remaining flour and mound the yeast into the centre. Fit the bucket into the breadmaker and set to the programme recommended in the manual (usually wholemeal). When ready, carefully shake the loaf out of the bucket on to a wire cooling rack and stand the right way up. If liked, brush with the selected glaze. Leave the loaf for at least an hour before cutting and/or removing the paddle if necessary.

FRENCH BREAD

A crisp and crusty bread with a fine, light texture, reminiscent of a French stick or baguette but shaped like a traditional loaf. As it stales fairly quickly, make it and eat it on the same day or bake it overnight so that it's fresh and warm and ready for breakfast with hot chocolate or mugs of café au lait.

Prepare as for either size Basic White Loaf, but omit the oil and dried milk. Select the French programme on your machine but otherwise bake as before and finish with a glaze or leave plain as preferred.

SOFT GRAIN BREAD

Prepare and bake as for either size Basic White Loaf, but use soft grain strong white bread flour with cracked grains of rye and wheat, instead of white.

SPELT FLOUR BREAD

A perfect specimen of a loaf, well-domed and shapely with a crisp golden crust and light texture.

225 g/8 oz/1½ cups (250 g/9 oz/1¾ cups) spelt flour

225 g/8 oz/1½ cups (250 g/9 oz/1¾ cups) strong white bread flour

275 ml/10 fl oz/1¼ cups (300 ml/11 fl oz/1⅜ cups) water

2 tbsp (2¼ tbsp) oil

2 tsp (2¼ tsp) salt

2 tsp (2¼ tsp) caster sugar

1 tbsp (1¼ tbsp) dried skimmed milk powder or granules

1¼ tsp (1½ tsp) instant or fast-acting dried yeast

glaze to taste (see page 19)

Thoroughly mix together the two flours. Pour the water into the breadmaker bucket, then add the oil and half the mixed flour. Sprinkle with the salt, sugar and dried milk. Cover with the remaining flour mix and mound the yeast into the centre. Fit the bucket into the breadmaker and set to the programme recommended in the manual (usually basic white or No 1). When ready, carefully shake the loaf out of the bucket on to a wire cooling rack and stand the right way up. If liked, brush with the selected glaze. Leave the loaf for at least an hour before cutting and/or removing the paddle if necessary.

HALF-AND-HALF SPELT FLOUR BREAD

Prepare and bake exactly as for Spelt Flour Bread, but use half strong brown (wholemeal) bread flour and half spelt flour.

BASIC BROWN LOAF

A country-style bread, heartily rustic, sturdy and with a distinctive home-made look. It's deeply wheaten-flavoured, splendidly-textured, crisply-crusted and suitable for anytime.

There is about three times as much fibre (bran) in strong brown flour as there is in white. This is known to inhibit the action of the gluten, especially when using a breadmaker set to the wholewheat programme. The loaf rises beautifully in the first instance and then, as the elastic gluten gets overstretched during the long kneading, rising, punching down and baking processes, the bread sinks back on itself, resulting in a bumpy top crust and sometimes even a sunken loaf. With the rapid programme, the loaf stays perfectly shaped and the top is attractively domed. The textures and tastes resulting from either programme are almost identical so the main difference is visual. Personally, I always opt for rapid.

The bran in wholewheat flour makes it more absorbent than white flour, which is reflected in the recipes by the increased amount of liquid used.

300 ml/11 fl oz/1⅜ cups (350 ml/12 fl oz/1½ cups) water

1½ tbsp (2 tbsp) oil

450 g/16 oz/3 cups (500 g/17½ oz/3½ cups) strong brown (wholemeal) bread flour

1¼ tsp (1½ tsp) salt

1 tbsp (1¼ tbsp) light brown soft sugar

1½ tbsp (2 tbsp) dried skimmed milk powder or granules

2 tsp (1 sachet) instant or fast-acting dried yeast

glaze to taste (see page 19)

Pour the water into the breadmaker bucket, then add the oil and half the flour. Sprinkle with the salt, sugar and dried milk. Cover with the remaining flour and mound the yeast into the centre. Fit the bucket into the bread machine and set to the programme recommended in the manual (usually wholewheat). When ready, carefully shake the loaf out of the bucket on to a wire cooling rack and stand the right way up. If liked, brush with the selected glaze. Leave the loaf for at least an hour before cutting and/or removing the paddle if necessary.

LIGHTLY LADEN BROWN LOAF

It is important to remember that brown bread is always denser than white, but its texture can be 'lightened' if a proportion of the flour is white.

Prepare and bake exactly as for Basic Brown Loaf, but use ⅔ strong brown bread flour and ⅓ strong white flour or half and half, as preferred.

BLINI BREAD

With a proportion of buckwheat flour (available from health food shops and some supermarkets), this almost taupe-coloured and rugged loaf is reminiscent of blinis, yeasted pancakes from Russia. These are served hot from the pan drenched in butter and accompanied by caviare or smoked salmon or both, and the obligatory soured cream or smetana, a Middle European cult. They are a gastronomic adventure, rich, succulent and unforgettably flavoured and you can approximate the whole thing by toasting thickish slices of this Blini Bread, dousing each one with butter so that it melts in and then eating with smoked salmon, soured cream or crème fraîche and maybe some pickled cucumber. You can also eat the toasted and buttered bread with eggs, cold roast meat or sausages like continental-style Viennas.

Native to Asia, buckwheat (other names are saracen corn or beechwheat) is the small fruit of the Fagopyrum esculentum shrub with pretty sweetly perfumed pink flowers. It is a member of the dock and rhubarb family. Interestingly, buckwheat is a fine source of vitamin B and also contains valuable protein, while its rutic acid content is said to be of benefit to those with coronary heart disease. It contains no wheat or gluten.

375 g/13 oz/2½ cups strong white bread flour

87 g/3 oz/⅝ cup buckwheat flour

275 ml/10 fl oz/1¼ cups water

2 tbsp oil

1½ tsp salt

3 tsp caster sugar

2 tbsp dried skimmed milk powder or granules

1 tsp instant or fast-acting dried yeast

glaze to taste (see page 19)

Thoroughly mix together the two flours. Pour the water into the breadmaker bucket, then add the oil and half the mixed flours. Sprinkle with the salt, sugar and dried milk. Cover with the remaining flour mix and mound the yeast into the centre. Fit the bucket into the breadmaker and set to the basic white or No 1 programme. When ready, carefully shake the loaf out of the bucket on to a wire cooling rack and stand the right way up. If liked, brush with the selected glaze. Leave the loaf for at least an hour before cutting and/or removing the paddle if necessary.

BARLEY BREAD

'Dark' white best describes the inside colour of this crusty, smooth and delicate-tasting bread. It cuts cleanly and evenly, has an almost cake-like texture, makes wholesome sandwiches and goes particularly well with soup. Barley is a nutritious grain that is said to discourage the liver from producing bad cholesterol, known as LDL (low density lipoprotein) by medical people. Barley is low in gluten.

Prepare and bake exactly as for Blini Bread, but using barley flour instead of buckwheat.

BROWN RICE BREAD

Doves Farm make their own flour from finely stoneground brown rice and, when combined with strong white, it makes a moist and subtle-tasting bread that cuts like a knife through butter. It has more body and character than the more familiar white rice flour used for thickening and sometimes puddings.

Prepare and bake exactly as for Blini Bread, but using brown rice flour instead of buckwheat.

SOYA FLOUR BREAD

A golden and dense-textured loaf that can be thinly sliced and left plain or toasted.

Prepare and bake exactly as for Blini Bread, but using soy flour (GM-free from health food shops) instead of buckwheat.

CHALLAH BREAD

Jewish Sabbath bread, enriched with eggs and delicately sweetened. It's light, lofty and moist, keeps fresh longer than most other breads, is perfectly textured and a beautiful foil for cold herring dishes like rollmops and the many other Scandinavian pickled herring varieties currently on the market in jars and cans. It also goes well with fish balls, fish terrines and fish cakes, with cold cooked meats and chopped liver (a favourite Jewish starter), liver pate and salamis. Authentic challah is long rather than tall and made from three or four ropes of dough plaited together or from one large rope coiled round on itself on the baking tray. These versions can be found on page 160 in the section on doughs.

2 medium eggs at kitchen temperature

water

2 tbsp (2¼ tbsp) oil

450 g/16 oz/3 cups (500 g/17½ oz/3½ cups) strong white bread flour

1 tsp (1½ tsp) salt

2 tbsp (3 tbsp) caster sugar

1½ tsp (1¾ tsp) instant or fast-acting dried yeast

beaten egg yolk to glaze

poppy seeds for sprinkling (optional)

Break the eggs into a measuring cup and make up to 275 ml/10 fl oz/1¼ cups (300 ml/11 fl oz/1⅜ cups) with water. Beat together lightly. Pour into the breadmaker bucket, then add the oil and half the flour. Sprinkle with the salt and sugar. Cover with the remaining flour and mound the yeast into the centre. Fit the bucket into the breadmaker and set to the basic white or No 1 programme. When ready, carefully shake the loaf out of the bucket on to a wire cooling rack and stand the right way up. Brush with egg yolk, then sprinkle with poppy seeds, if using. Leave the loaf for at least an hour before cutting and/or removing the paddle if necessary.

seed and nut breads

RYE AND ANISEED BREAD

A little gem of a loaf, reminiscent of the firm and semi-dark breads eaten in northern and central Europe. It domes perfectly, the texture is smooth, the colour is light golden brown and the taste expensive. Considering it is well-endowed with rye flour, the bread is surprisingly light.

225 g/8 oz/1½ cups rye flour

225 g/8 oz /1½ cups strong white bread flour

1 tbsp black treacle

water

2 tbsp oil

1½ tsp salt

1 tbsp soft light brown sugar

2 tbsp aniseeds

1½ tsp instant or fast-acting dried yeast

glaze to taste (see page 19)

Thoroughly mix together the two flours. Put the treacle in a measuring cup and stir until smooth with a little hot water. Top up with cold water to make 275 ml/ 10 fl oz/1¼ cups. Pour into the breadmaker bucket, then add the oil and half the mixed flour. Sprinkle with the salt, sugar and aniseeds. Cover with the remaining flour mix and mound the yeast into the centre. Fit the bucket into the breadmaker and set to the rapid programme. When ready, carefully shake the loaf out of the bucket on to a wire cooling rack and stand the right way up. If liked, brush with the selected glaze. Leave the loaf for at least an hour before cutting and/or removing the paddle if necessary.

CARAWAY SEED BREAD

Deli style, the 'in' bread for hot salt beef or tongue sarnies with mustard and pickled cucumbers and also those monster double and triple decker sandwiches eaten all over North America with French fries and salad.

275 ml/10 fl oz/1¼ cups (300 ml/11 fl oz/1⅜ cups) water

1 tbsp (1¼ tbsp) oil

450 g/16 oz/3 cups (500 g/17½ oz/3½ cups) strong white bread flour

1½ tsp (2 tsp) salt

2 tsp (2½ tsp) caster sugar

2 tbsp (2½ tsp) caraway seeds

1 tbsp (1¼ tbsp) dried skimmed milk powder or granules (optional)

1½ tsp (1¾ tsp) instant or fast-acting dried yeast

glaze to taste (see page 19)

Pour the water into the breadmaker bucket, then add the oil and half the flour. Sprinkle with the salt, sugar, caraway seeds and dried milk, if using. Cover with the remaining flour and mound the yeast into the centre. Fit the bucket into the breadmaker and set to the programme recommended in the manual (usually basic white or No 1). When ready, carefully shake the loaf out of the bucket on to a wire cooling rack and stand the right way up. If liked, brush with the selected glaze. Leave the loaf for at least an hour before cutting and/or removing the paddle if necessary.

BRONZED SESAME BREAD

This bread is unmistakenly Middle Eastern by adoption and is stunning with a meze, the typical and gargantuan hors d'œuvres of the region with its creamy dips and hot and cold dishes of beans, aubergines, stuffed vine leaves, hummus, falafel, stuffed olives, fried liver, small kebabs of lamb and chicken and mixed salads.

275 ml/10 fl oz/1¼ cups (300 ml/11 fl oz/1⅜ cups) water

1 tbsp (1¼ tbsp) toasted sesame oil

450 g/16 oz/3 cups (500 g/17½ oz/3½ cups) soft grain strong white bread flour

1½ tsp (2 tsp) salt

2 tsp (2½ tsp) soft brown sugar

1 tbsp (1¼ tbsp) dried skimmed milk powder or granules

4 tbsp (5 tbsp) lightly toasted white sesame seeds

1½ tsp (1¾ tsp) instant or fast-acting dried yeast

glaze to taste (see page 19)

Pour the water into the breadmaker bucket, then add the oil and half the flour. Sprinkle with the salt, sugar, dried milk and sesame seeds. Cover with the remaining flour and mound the yeast into the centre. Fit the bucket into the breadmaker and set to the programme recommended in the manual (usually basic white or No 1). When ready, carefully shake the loaf out of the bucket on to a wire cooling rack and stand the right way up. If liked, brush with the selected glaze. Leave the loaf for at least an hour before cutting and/or removing the paddle if necessary.

PISTACHIO BREAD WITH GRAPE-SEED OIL AND CARDAMOM

Well-endowed with bright green pistachios and distinctively flavoured with golden-green grapeseed oil and cardamom, the bread is a kind of east-west triumph, a handsome giant and a subtle and discreet accompaniment to roast lamb and lamb casseroles, all things vegetarian, cream cheeses and Greek Haloumi or Feta cheeses, and eggs in every shape or form. The ground cardamom is available from Indian food shops.

75 g/3 oz/¾ cup shelled but unskinned pistachios

275 ml/10 fl oz/1¼ cups water

2 tbsp grapeseed oil

450 g/16 oz/3 cups soft grain strong white bread flour

1½ tsp salt

2 tsp caster sugar

1 tsp ground cardamom

1½ tsp instant or fast-acting dried yeast

glaze to taste (see page 19)

Blanch the pistachios by placing them in a basin and covering with boiling water. Leave for 4–5 minutes, then drain. Slide the skins off with a clean teatowel and discard. Leave the nuts aside. Pour the water into the breadmaker bucket, then add the oil and half the flour. Sprinkle with the salt, sugar and cardamom. Cover with the remaining flour and mound the yeast into the centre. Fit the bucket into the breadmaker and set to the programme recommended in the manual (either special if the machine has this setting or basic white or No 1). Add the pistachios according to the manual's instructions, usually at the beginning or the middle of the second kneading or when the machine bleeps. When ready, carefully shake the loaf out of the bucket on to a wire cooling rack and stand the right way up. If liked, brush with the selected glaze. Leave the loaf for at least an hour before cutting and/or removing the paddle if necessary.

PINE NUT AND SAFFRON BREAD

An elegant contribution and an asset to have on hand for special guests. The bread is smooth and mellow, original, shapely and immaculately turned out.

50 g/2 oz/⅜ cup pine nuts

½ tsp saffron strands

1 tbsp boiling water

275 ml/10 fl oz/1¼ cups cold water less 1 tbsp

2 tbsp oil

450 g/16 oz/3 cups strong white bread flour

1½ tsp salt

2 tsp light brown soft sugar

1½ tsp instant or fast-acting dried yeast

glaze to taste (see page 19)

Toast the pine nuts by stirring constantly in a non-stick frying pan over a low heat until lightly golden. Set aside. Put the saffron in a small bowl. Mix in the boiling water and leave aside until cold. Pour the cold water into the breadmaker bucket, then add the oil, saffron and its water with half the flour. Sprinkle with the salt and sugar. Cover with the remaining flour and mound the yeast into the centre. Fit the bucket into the breadmaker and set to the programme recommended in the manual (either special if the machine has this setting or basic white or No 1). Add the pine nuts according to the manual's instructions, usually at the beginning or the middle of the second kneading or when the machine bleeps. When ready, carefully shake the loaf out of the bucket on to a wire cooling rack and stand the right way up. If liked, brush with the selected glaze. Leave the loaf for at least an hour before cutting and/or removing the paddle if necessary.

MILD CURRY BREAD WITH YOGHURT AND CASHEWS

A gentle bread, well-suited to vegetarian food, salads, curries, boiled eggs and creamy cheeses. The slightly bitey texture comes from the country grain flour and the nuts.

225 g/8 oz/1½ cups strong white bread flour

225 g/8 oz/1½ cups country grain strong white bread flour

5 tbsp low-fat set yoghurt

water

2 tbsp oil

2 tbsp korma curry powder

50 g/2 oz/⅝ cup salted cashews, broken into pieces

2 tsp salt

2 tsp soft brown sugar

1½ tsp instant or fast-acting dried yeast

glaze to taste (see page 19)

Thoroughly mix together the two flours. Make up the yoghurt to 275 ml/10 fl oz/ 1¼ cups with water and pour into the breadmaker bucket. Add the oil and half the mixed flour. Sprinkle with the curry powder, cashews, salt and sugar. Cover with the remaining flour mix and mound the yeast into the centre. Fit the bucket into the breadmaker and set to the programme recommended in the manual (usually basic white or No 1). When ready, carefully shake the loaf out of the bucket on to a wire cooling rack and stand the right way up. If liked, brush with the selected glaze. Leave the loaf for at least an hour before cutting and/or removing the paddle if necessary.

SIX SEED BREAD

Brimming with seeds and what can best be described as 'continental' in colour and taste, this dark bread is full of crunch and good health, much lighter in texture than other members of its fairly close and seedy family. It's reminiscent of the breads from individual bakery shops you find in Holland, Belgium and Germany and is a big hit with everyone who tries it.

300 ml/11 fl oz/1⅜ cups (350 ml/12 fl oz/1½ cups) water

2 tbsp (2¼ tbsp) oil

450 g/16 oz/3 cups (500 g/17½ oz/3½ cups) country grain strong brown bread flour

1½ tsp (1¾ tsp) salt

2 tsp (2½ tsp) soft brown sugar

2 tbsp (2½ tbsp) dried skimmed milk powder or granules

2 tbsp (2½ tbsp) sunflower seeds

1 tbsp (1¼ tbsp) dark poppy seeds

1 tsp (1¼ tsp) EACH caraway or aniseed, cumin, fennel and air-dried black onion seeds

1½ tsp (1¾ tsp) instant or fast-acting dried yeast

glaze to taste (see page 19)

Pour the water into the breadmaker bucket, then add the oil and half the flour. Sprinkle with the salt, sugar, dried milk and all the seeds. Cover with the remaining flour and mound the yeast into the centre. Fit the bucket into the breadmaker and set to the programme recommended in the manually (usually wholemeal). When ready, carefully shake the loaf out of the bucket on to a wire cooling rack and stand the right way up. If liked, brush with the selected glaze. Leave the loaf for at least an hour before cutting and/or removing the paddle if necessary.

BRAZIL NUT AND NUTMEG BREAD

A most personable and well-balanced loaf with a crisp texture and the merest trace of fresh nutmeg in the background.

275 ml/10 fl oz/1¼ cups water

2 tbsp oil

450 g/16 oz/3 cups soft grain strong white bread flour

1½ tsp salt

2 tsp caster sugar

1 tsp freshly grated nutmeg

1½ tsp instant or fast-acting dried yeast

75 g/3 oz/⅞ cup brazil nuts, coarsely chopped

glaze to taste (see page 19)

Pour the water into the breadmaker bucket, then add the oil and half the flour. Sprinkle with the salt, sugar and nutmeg. Cover with the remaining flour and mound the yeast into the centre. Fit the bucket into the breadmaker and set to the programme recommended in the manual (either special if the machine has this setting or basic white or No 1). Add the brazil nuts according to the manual's instructions, usually at the beginning or the middle of the second kneading or when the machine bleeps. When ready, carefully shake the loaf out of the bucket on to a wire cooling rack and stand the right way up. If liked, brush with the selected glaze. Leave the loaf for at least an hour before cutting and/or removing the paddle if necessary.

PLAIN WALNUT BREAD

A fashionable bread, very much part of the trendy restaurant scene and always popular with the dining-out crowd. Milder pecan nuts may be used, if preferred.

300 g/11 oz/2 cups strong white bread flour

150 g/5¼ oz/1 cup country grain strong brown bread flour with malted wheat flakes

300 ml/11 fl oz/1⅜ cups water

2 tbsp oil

1¼ tsp salt

1 tbsp light brown soft sugar

100 g/3½ oz/¾ cup walnut pieces

1½ tsp instant or fast-acting dried yeast

glaze to taste (see page 19)

Thoroughly mix together the two flours. Pour the water into the breadmaker bucket, then add the oil and half the mixed flour. Sprinkle with the salt and sugar. Cover with the remaining flour mix and mound the yeast into the centre. Fit the bucket into the breadmaker and set to the programme recommended in the manual (either special if the machine has this setting or basic white or No 1). Add the walnuts according to the manual's instructions, usually at the beginning or the middle of the second kneading or when the machine bleeps. When ready, carefully shake the loaf out of the bucket on to a wire cooling rack and stand the right way up. If liked, brush with the selected glaze. Leave the loaf for at least an hour before cutting and/or removing the paddle if necessary.

BUTTER-FRIED WALNUT AND PARMESAN BREAD

Using walnuts and Parmesan cheese, ingredients familiar to northern Italians and so revered in Emilia Romagna and Tuscany, the loaf is a handsome, up-market affair and the sort of bread one could serve at formal dinner parties or casual meals round the kitchen table. It's a good mixer, so does well with starters, soups and cheese.

100 g/3½ oz/⅞ cup walnut pieces

25 g/1 oz/⅛ cup unsalted butter

275 ml/10 fl oz/1¼ cups water

1 tbsp olive oil

450 g/16 oz/3 cups strong white bread flour

1½ tsp salt

2 tsp caster sugar

2 tbsp dried skimmed milk powder or granules

4 tbsp freshly grated Parmesan cheese

1¼ tsp instant or fast-acting dried yeast

glaze to taste (see page 19)

Break up the walnuts into smaller pieces with your fingers and fry slowly in a small saucepan with the butter until golden. Leave to cool. Pour the water into the breadmaker bucket, then add the oil and half the flour. Sprinkle with the salt, sugar, dried milk and Parmesan followed by the walnuts and the butter in which they were fried. Cover with the remaining flour and mound the yeast into the centre. Fit the bucket into the breadmaker and set to the programme recommended in the manual (usually basic white or No 1). When ready, carefully shake the loaf out of the bucket on to a wire cooling rack and stand the right way up. If liked, brush with the selected glaze. Leave the loaf for at least an hour before cutting and/or removing the paddle if necessary.

TOASTED MACADAMIA BREAD

This is a bread to make when you're in an extravagant mood. It is divinely rich and classy, woven with pieces of eastern Australia's costly and quite exquisite macadamia nuts. It goes equally well with sweet or savoury foods and has an expensive and luxurious feel to it.

75 g/3 oz/¾ cup macadamia nuts

275 ml/10 fl oz/1¼ cups water

3 tbsp melted butter

450 g/16 oz/3 cups strong white bread flour

1½ tsp salt

2 tsp caster sugar

1½ tsp instant or fast-acting dried yeast

glaze to taste (see page 19)

Cut the nuts into chunky pieces and brown slowly in a dry frying pan, stirring often to prevent burning. Leave aside until cold. Pour the water into the breadmaker bucket, then add the butter and half the flour. Sprinkle with the salt and sugar. Cover with the remaining flour and mound the yeast into the centre. Fit the bucket into the breadmaker and set to the programme recommended in the manual (either special if the machine has this setting or basic white or No 1). Add the nuts according to the manual's instructions, usually at the beginning or the middle of the second kneading or when the machine bleeps. When ready, carefully shake the loaf out of the bucket on to a wire cooling rack and stand the right way up. If liked, brush with the selected glaze. Leave the loaf for at least an hour before cutting and/or removing the paddle if necessary.

BROWNED ALMOND AND ORANGE BREAD

Fragrant and sophisticated, this bread is designed to complement most members of the fish family with a deep flavour – tuna, winter carp, sardines, mackerel and herring – and chicken stews and casseroles cooked with fruity red or white wine and assorted fresh herbs.

275 ml/10 fl oz/1¼ cups water

2 tbsp oil

450 g/16 oz/3 cups soft grain strong white bread flour

1½ tsp salt

2 tsp caster sugar

1 tsp very finely grated orange peel

1½ tsp instant or fast-acting dried yeast

100 g/3½ oz/¾ cup blanched and toasted almonds, coarsely chopped

glaze to taste (see page 19)

Pour the water into the breadmaker bucket, then add the oil and half the flour. Sprinkle with the salt, sugar and orange peel. Cover with the remaining flour and mound the yeast into the centre. Fit the bucket into the breadmaker and set to the programme recommended in the manual (either special if the machine has this setting or basic white or No 1). Add the almonds according to the manual's instructions, usually at the beginning or the middle of the second kneading or when the machine bleeps. When ready, carefully shake the loaf out of the bucket on to a wire cooling rack and stand the right way up. If liked, brush with the selected glaze. Leave the loaf for at least an hour before cutting and/or removing the paddle if necessary.

speciality flavoured breads

SPECIALITY FLAVOURED BREADS

If you intend making any of the larger loaves with the measures given in brackets in some of the recipes (not all lend themselves to adaptation), ensure your breadmaker will take 500 g/17½ oz/3⅜ cups of flour in addition to all the other ingredients included before you start. Additionally, if you are using the delay programme which works overnight, do NOT use perishable ingredients such as eggs, fresh milk and butter. Always be guided by your instruction manual.

Where oil has been used in the recipes, melted unsalted butter or margarine may be substituted.

FULL ENGLISH BREAKFAST BREAD

A wonderful return to traditional values and a morning glory when accompanied by sausages, eggs, tomatoes, baked beans, bacon, black pudding and mushrooms. It's great fried, or try it thickly sliced, toasted and topped with Cheddar cheese and pickle for a quick lunch or supper.

2 medium eggs, at room temperature

2 tbsp (3 tbsp) brown ketchup

water

2 tbsp (2¼ tbsp) oil

450 g/16 oz/3 cups (500 g/17½ oz/3½ cups) strong white bread flour

4 tbsp (5 tbsp) bacon-flavoured bits, available in tubs or jars

1½ tsp (1¾ tsp) salt

1 tsp (1½ tsp) caster sugar

2 tbsp (2½ tbsp) dried skimmed milk powder or granules

1½ tsp (1¾ tsp) instant or fast-acting dried yeast

glaze to taste (see page 19)

Break the eggs into a measuring cup. Add the ketchup and make up to 275 ml/ 10 fl oz/1¼ cups (300 ml/11 fl oz/1⅜ cups) with water. Lightly beat and pour into the breadmaker bucket. Add the oil and half the flour. Sprinkle with the bacon bits, salt, sugar and dried milk. Cover with the remaining flour and mound the yeast into the centre. Fit the bucket into the breadmaker and set to the basic white or No 1 programme. When ready, carefully shake the loaf out of the bucket on to a wire cooling rack and stand the right way up. If liked, brush with the selected glaze. Leave the loaf for at least an hour before cutting and/or removing the paddle if necessary.

HUNGARIAN BREAD WITH MUSTARD AND PAPRIKA

The idea for this bread came from a leaflet I found in Fauchon, Paris's equivalent of London's Fortnum & Mason. It was a listing and description of the different mustards available in this dream of a food shop. There must have been at least twenty and one called Hongroise stayed in my mind because it was original and clever, the addition of paprika to mustard adding a simple yet unique touch. Used in bread, it has a delicate charm and provides a hint of times past, reminiscent of the tastes and aromas of the old Austro-Hungarian Empire and all its regal splendours. It's a treasure toasted and topped with fried mushrooms heated with double cream, fried chicken or turkey livers treated in the same way, or simply on the side with gammon steaks or roast pork.

275 ml/10 fl oz/1¼ cups (300 ml/11 fl oz/1⅜ cups) water less 1 tbsp (4 tsp)

2 tbsp (2¼ tbsp) oil

450 g/16 oz/3 cups (500 g/17½ oz/3½ cups) soft grain strong white bread flour

2 tsp (2¼ tsp) salt

2 tsp (2¼ tsp) caster sugar

3 tsp (3½ tsp) paprika

½–¾ tsp (¾–1 tsp) cayenne pepper

1 tbsp (1¼ tbsp) dried skimmed milk powder or granules

4 tsp (5 tsp) Dijon mustard

⅓ tsp (½ tsp) instant or fast-acting dried yeast

glaze to taste (see page 19)

Pour the water into the breadmaker bucket, then add the oil and half the flour. Sprinkle with the salt, sugar, paprika, cayenne pepper and dried milk. Add the mustard. Cover with the remaining flour and mound the yeast into the centre. Fit the bucket into the breadmaker and set to the programme recommended in the manual (usually basic white or No 1). When ready, carefully shake the loaf out of the bucket on to a wire cooling rack and stand the right way up. If liked, brush with the selected glaze. Leave the loaf for at least an hour before cutting and/or removing the paddle if necessary.

POLENTA BREAD WITH OLIVE OIL

With a whisper of Italy, this golden-hearted loaf is impressive and flavourful and companionable with any mixed antipasti and those hearty country soups packed with pasta and every vegetable under the sun – minestrone springs readily to mind. For fast pizzas, cut the loaf downwards from top to bottom to make long slices, spread with tomato paste or tapenade, cover with slices of tomato, then Mozzarella, stud with olives and brown under the grill.

400 g/14 oz/2¾ cups strong white bread flour

50 g/2 oz/¼ cup coarse polenta

275 ml/10 fl oz/1¼ cups water

2 tbsp extra virgin olive oil

2 tsp salt

1 tsp caster sugar

2 tbsp dried skimmed milk powder or granules

1½ tsp instant or fast-acting dried yeast

glaze to taste (see page 19)

Mix together the flour and polenta. Pour the water into the breadmaker bucket, then add the oil and half the flour and polenta mixture. Sprinkle with the salt, sugar and dried milk. Cover with the remaining flour mix and mound the yeast into the centre. Fit the bucket into the breadmaker and set to the programme recommended in the manual (usually basic white or No 1). When ready, carefully shake the loaf out of the bucket on to a wire cooling rack and stand the right way up. If liked, brush with the selected glaze. Leave the loaf for at least an hour before cutting and/or removing the paddle if necessary.

GARLIC BUTTER BREAD

The best! Unusually soft-crusted and tender, the garlic and butter blend cosily together to produce a loaf for a sophisticated meal of seafood, grilled fish fillets, roasted vegetables, chicken or veal Cordon Bleu and cheese souffles or plain omelettes. It's wonderful thickly sliced and toasted, then covered with grilled tomatoes sprinkled with parsley and a dusting of grated lemon peel, or with fried mushrooms.

2 tbsp (2½ tbsp) unsalted butter

275 ml/10 fl oz/1¼ cups (300 ml/11 fl oz/1⅜ cups) water

2 tbsp (2½ tbsp) garlic purée

450 g/16 oz/3 cups (500 g/17½ oz/3½ cups) strong white bread flour

2 tsp (2½ tsp) salt

2 tsp (2½ tsp) caster sugar

1 tbsp (1¼ tbsp) dried skimmed milk powder or granules

1¼ tsp (1½ tsp) instant or fast-acting dried yeast

glaze to taste (see page 19)

Melt the butter gently in a saucepan or in a dish in the microwave on the defrost setting. Pour the water into the breadmaker bucket, then add the butter, garlic purée and half the flour. Sprinkle with the salt, sugar and dried milk. Cover with the remaining flour and mound the yeast into the centre. Fit the bucket into the breadmaker and set to the programme recommended in the manual (usually basic white or No 1). When ready, carefully shake the loaf out of the bucket on to a wire cooling rack and stand the right way up. If liked, brush with the selected glaze. Leave the loaf for at least an hour before cutting and/or removing the paddle if necessary.

SPICY YOGHURT BREAD

A gentle bread, well-suited to vegetarian food, curries, boiled eggs and cream cheese. The slightly bitey texture comes from the country grain flour.

225 g/8 oz/1½ cups strong white bread flour

225 g/8 oz/1½ cups country grain strong white bread flour

5 tbsp low-fat set yoghurt

water

2 tbsp oil

2 tbsp korma curry powder

2 tsp salt

2 tsp soft brown sugar

1½ tsp instant or fast-acting dried yeast

glaze to taste (see page 19)

Thoroughly mix together the two flours. Make up the yoghurt to 275 ml/10 fl oz/1¼ cups with water and pour into the breadmaker bucket. Add the oil and half the mixed flours. Sprinkle with the curry powder, salt and sugar. Cover with the remaining flour mix and mound the yeast into the centre. Fit the bucket into the breadmaker and set to the programme recommended in the manual (usually basic white or No 1). When ready, carefully shake the loaf out of the bucket on to a wire cooling rack and stand the right way up. If liked, brush with the selected glaze. Leave the loaf for at least an hour before cutting and/or removing the paddle if necessary.

ONION BHAJIA BREAD

This bread instantly says Indian and is almost a replica, in bread form, of one of Britain's most popular starters. To give it authenticity, some gram (chickpea) flour has been included. The spicing is classic and the texture light and appetising. A fine bread for home-style tandoori chicken and fish curries.

400 g/14 oz/2¾ cups strong white bread flour

50 g/2 oz/½ cup gram flour

6 tbsp dried onions

275 ml/10 fl oz/1¼ cups water

1 tbsp oil

2 tsp salt

2 tsp caster sugar

3 tsp garam masala

1 tsp powdered ginger

½ tsp ground cumin

1½ tsp instant or fast-acting dried yeast

glaze to taste (see page 19)

Thoroughly mix together the two flours. Dry-fry the onions in a frying pan until golden-brown, moving them about frequently to prevent burning. Take out of the pan and cool on a plate. Pour the water into the breadmaker bucket, then add the oil and half the mixed flours. Sprinkle with the salt, sugar, garam masala, ginger, cumin and fried onions. Cover with the remaining flour mixture and mound the yeast into the centre. Fit the bucket into the breadmaker and set to the programme recommended in the manual (usually basic white or No 1). When ready, carefully shake the loaf out of the bucket on to a wire cooling rack and stand the right way up. If liked, brush with the selected glaze. Leave the loaf for at least an hour before cutting and/or removing the paddle if necessary.

CANTON BLACK BEAN BREAD

Unmistakably Chinese in character with an exotic and almost mystical after-taste. Eat with stir-fries instead of rice or noodles or with any sweet-sour dishes.

225 g/8 oz/1½ cups strong white bread flour

225 g/8 oz/1½ cups strong brown (wholemeal) bread flour

275 ml/10 fl oz/1¼ cups water plus 1tbsp

1 tbsp oil

1½ tsp salt

2 tsp caster sugar

1 tbsp dried skimmed milk powder or granules

4 tbsp stir-fry Canton Black Bean Sauce (Blue Dragon sachet)

1½ tsp instant or fast-acting dried yeast

glaze to taste (see page 19)

Thoroughly mix together the two flours. Pour the water into the breadmaker bucket, then add the oil and half the mixed flours. Sprinkle with the salt, sugar and dried milk and spoon the stir-fry sauce over the top. Cover with the remaining flour mix and mound the yeast into the centre. Fit the bucket into the breadmaker and set to the programme recommended in the manual (usually basic white or No 1). When ready, carefully shake the loaf out of the bucket on to a wire cooling rack and stand the right way up. If liked, brush with the selected glaze. Leave the loaf for at least an hour before cutting and/or removing the paddle if necessary.

INDONESIAN SATAY BREAD

Hints of warm Oriental fragrances emerge triumphant from this Far Eastern-tasting bread, perfect with kebabs of pork or beef or any Indonesian meat or chicken curry.

275 ml/10 fl oz/1¼ cups water

1 tbsp oil

450 g/16 oz/3 cups soft grain strong white bread flour

1½ tsp salt

2 tsp soft brown sugar

1 tbsp dried skimmed milk powder or granules

4 tbsp stir-fry Orange and Green Ginger Sauce (Blue Dragon sachet)

1½ tsp instant or fast-acting dried yeast

glaze to taste (see page 19)

Pour the water into the breadmaker bucket, then add the oil and half the flour. Sprinkle with the salt, sugar and dried milk and spoon the stir-fry sauce over. Cover with the remaining flour and mound the yeast into the centre. Fit the bucket into the breadmaker and set to the programme recommended in the manual (usually basic white or No 1). When ready, carefully shake the loaf out of the bucket on to a wire cooling rack and stand the right way up. If liked, brush with the selected glaze. Leave the loaf for at least an hour before cutting and/or removing the paddle if necessary.

THAI RED CURRY AND COCONUT BREAD

Anything Thai these days is considered trendy and this spicy bread, with a bit of heat to it, is no exception. The lemon grass has the effect of making the bread refreshing and cool and the loaf is highly recommended for summer sarnies filled with cold roast chicken or pork and green salad. It also complements chicken soup and Thai curries nicely and may also be eaten with fishcakes.

150 ml/5 fl oz/⅝ cup water less 2 tbsp

150 ml/5 fl oz/⅝ cup canned coconut milk

1 tbsp oil

450 g/16 oz/3 cups strong white bread flour

1½ tsp salt

2 tsp caster sugar

4 tbsp stir-fry Thai Red Curry Sauce (Blue Dragon sachet)

1½ tsp instant or fast-acting dried yeast

glaze to taste (see page 19)

Pour the water and coconut milk into the breadmaker bucket, then add the oil and half the flour. Sprinkle with the salt and sugar and spoon the curry sauce over the top. Cover with the remaining flour and mound the yeast into the centre. Fit the bucket into the breadmaker and set to the programme recommended in the manual (usually basic white or No 1). When ready, carefully shake the loaf out of the bucket on to a wire cooling rack and stand the right way up. If liked, brush with the selected glaze. Leave the loaf for at least an hour before cutting and/or removing the paddle if necessary.

MEDITERRANEAN BLACK OLIVE AND ANCHOVY BREAD

A classy and distinctive bread, full of Mediterranean warmth and character from the addition of tapenade, a flavourful black olive and anchovy paste. It's pure sunshine with roasted vegetables or chunky salads as a starter, with strong French blue or Camembert cheese to end.

275 ml/10 fl oz/1¼ cups (300 ml/11 fl oz/1⅜ cups) water

3 tbsp (3½ tbsp) tapenade paste

1 tbsp (1¼ tbsp) oil

450 g/16 oz/3 cups (500 g/17½ oz/3½ cups) strong white bread flour

1½ tsp (1¾ tsp) salt

2 tsp (2½ tsp) caster sugar

1¼ tsp (1½ tsp) instant or fast-acting dried yeast

glaze to taste (see page 19)

Pour the water into the breadmaker bucket, then add the tapenade paste, oil and half the flour. Sprinkle with the salt and sugar. Cover with the remaining flour and mound the yeast into the centre. Fit the bucket into the breadmaker and set to the programme recommended in the manual (usually basic white or No 1). When ready, carefully shake the loaf out of the bucket on to a wire cooling rack and stand the right way up. If liked, brush with the selected glaze. Leave the loaf for at least an hour before cutting and/or removing the paddle if necessary.

EGG MAYONNAISE BREAD

A lovely bread this, the taste described by one visitor as 'like a good wine'. Certainly it's heaven-sent for smoked salmon, trout and mackerel and equally appealing with grilled oily fish and fresh tuna. For a touch of nostalgia, slice the loaf thinly and sandwich together with hard-boiled eggs and cress and the obligatory salad cream.

225 g/8 oz/1½ cups
(250 g/9 oz/1¾ cups)
strong white bread flour

225 g/8 oz/1½ cups
(250 g/9 oz/1¾ cups)
strong brown (wholemeal)
bread flour

1 medium (1 large) egg,
at kitchen temperature

water

3 tbsp (3½ tbsp) top-
quality mayonnaise,
preferably with olive oil

2 tsp (2½ tsp) salt

2 tsp (2½ tsp) caster
sugar

1 tbsp (1¼ tbsp) dried
skimmed milk powder or
granules

1¼ tsp (1½ tsp) instant or
fast-acting dried yeast

glaze to taste (see
page 19)

Thoroughly mix together the two flours. Break the egg into a measuring cup and make up to 275 ml/10 fl oz /1¼ cups (300 ml/11 fl oz/1⅜ cups) with water. Pour the into the breadmaker bucket, then add the mayonnaise and half the mixed flours. Sprinkle with the salt, sugar and dried milk. Cover with the remaining flour mix and mound the yeast into the centre. Fit the bucket into the breadmaker and set to the programme recommended in the manual (usually basic white or No 1). When ready, carefully shake the loaf out of the bucket on to a wire cooling rack and stand the right way up. If liked, brush with the selected glaze. Leave the loaf for at least an hour before cutting and/or removing the paddle if necessary.

GARLIC AND LEMON MAYONNAISE BREAD

Smooth and chic, this recipe is based on an old charmer from the South of France, a rich mayonnaise sauce highlighted with garlic and woven into the bread like strands of silken thread.

Prepare and bake exactly as for Egg Mayonnaise Bread, but use garlic salt instead of plain and include with it ½ tsp (¾ tsp) finely grated lemon rind.

FRENCH ONION BREAD

The daddy of all breads. Splendid with everything, but it makes the snappiest sandwiches ever with steaks, roast meats and tongue – or cheese with salad for vegetarians – and even lifts Spam to the dizzy heights of respectability. And if you make French onion soup at home, put thick slices of this bread on top of each bowl before smothering with cheese and browning under the grill. Heaven!

450 g/16 oz/3 cups soft grain soft white flour less 4 tbsp

4 tbsp (about 39 g packet) French onion soup mix

275 ml/10 fl oz/1¼ cups water

1 tbsp oil

1 tsp salt

2 tsp soft brown sugar

1 tbsp dried skimmed milk powder or granules

1 tsp instant or fast-acting dried yeast

glaze to taste (see page 19)

Mix together the flour and soup mix. Pour the water into the breadmaker bucket, then add the oil and half the flour mixture. Sprinkle with the salt, sugar and dried milk. Cover with the remaining flour mix and mound the yeast into the centre. Fit the bucket into the breadmaker and set to the programme recommended in the manual (usually basic white or No 1). When ready, carefully shake the loaf out of the bucket on to a wire cooling rack and stand the right way up. If liked, brush with the selected glaze. Leave the loaf for at least an hour before cutting and/or removing the paddle if necessary.

ITALIAN BREAD

Smart and sophisticated with that heady kick-back of basil, so typical of Italian food. This bread is likely to go down in culinary history as a classic and is a tribute to the Italian food company Sacla, makers of fine quality pesto, who entertained me so handsomely a few years ago, taking time to show me round their pesto plant with its mountains of bright green basil, waxy pine nuts and fresh Parmesan cheese.

275 ml/10 fl oz/1¼ cups (300 ml/11 fl oz/1⅜ cups) water

4 tbsp (4½ tbsp) pesto

1 tbsp (1¼ tbsp) olive oil

450 g/16 oz /3 cups (500 g/17½ oz/3½ cups) strong white bread flour

1½ tsp (1¾ tsp) salt

2 tsp (2¼ tsp) caster sugar

2 tsp (2½ tsp) dried basil

1½ tsp (1¾ tsp) instant or fast-acting dried yeast

glaze to taste (see page 19)

Pour the water into the breadmaker bucket, then add the pesto and oil and half the flour. Sprinkle with the salt, sugar and basil. Cover with the remaining flour and mound the yeast into the centre. Fit the bucket into the breadmaker and set to the programme recommended in the manual (usually basic white or No 1). When ready, carefully shake the loaf out of the bucket on to a wire cooling rack and stand the right way up. If liked, brush with the selected glaze. Leave the loaf for at least an hour before cutting and/or removing the paddle if necessary.

COARSEGRAIN MUSTARD BREAD

A snazzy and adaptable bread, this fits in happily with any cooked breakfast, especially smoked haddock and poached eggs, and makes a piquant base for Welsh rarebit. Leftovers, if there are any, can be converted into crumbs and used for stuffing and crusty toppings.

275 ml/10 fl oz/1¼ cups
(300 ml/11 fl oz/1⅜ cups)
water

4 tbsp (4½ tbsp)
coarsegrain mustard

1 tbsp (1¼ tbsp) oil

450 g/16 oz/3 cups
(500 g/17½ oz/3½ cups)
strong white bread flour

1½ tsp (1¾ tsp) salt

2 tsp (2½ tsp) soft brown
sugar

1 tbsp (1¼ tbsp) dried
skimmed milk powder or
granules

1¼ tsp (1½ tsp) instant or
fast-acting dried yeast

glaze to taste (see
page 19)

Pour the water into the breadmaker bucket, then add the mustard, oil and half the flour. Sprinkle with the salt, sugar and dried milk. Cover with the remaining flour and mound the yeast into the centre. Fit the bucket into the breadmaker and set to the programme recommended in the manual (usually basic white or No 1). When ready, carefully shake the loaf out of the bucket on to a wire cooling rack and stand the right way up. If liked, brush with the selected glaze. Leave the loaf for at least an hour before cutting and/or removing the paddle if necessary.

SUNDRIED TOMATO AND GARLIC BREAD

Up there with the best of them, this bread has spicy Italian panache and its own striking personality. It's appetising with Italian cold salamis and meats, mixed leaf salads, sautéed wild mushrooms and mild Italian cheeses.

150 ml/5 fl oz/⅝ cup (200 ml/7 fl oz/⅞ cup) tomato juice

water

1 tbsp (1¼ tbsp) sundried tomato paste

2 tbsp (2½ tbsp) extra virgin olive oil

450 g/16 oz/3 cups (500 g/17½ oz/3½ cups) strong white bread flour

1½ tsp (1¾ tsp) onion salt

2 tsp (2½ tsp) caster sugar

1 tbsp (1¼ tbsp) dried skimmed milk powder or granules

1 tbsp (1¼ tbsp) Schwartz Garlic and Mushroom Pasta Sauce Seasoning or 1 tsp EACH dried basil, rosemary and paprika

1½ tsp (1¾ tsp) instant or fast-acting dried yeast

glaze to taste (see page 19)

Make up the tomato juice to 275 ml/10 fl oz/1¼ cups (300 ml/11 fl oz/ 1⅜ cups) with water. Pour into the breadmaker bucket, then add the tomato paste, oil and half the flour. Sprinkle with the salt, sugar, dried milk and pasta seasoning. Cover with the remaining flour and mound the yeast into the centre. Fit the bucket into the breadmaker and set to the programme recommended in the manual (usually basic white or No 1). When ready, carefully shake the loaf out of the bucket on to a wire cooling rack and stand the right way up. If liked, brush with the selected glaze. Leave the loaf for at least an hour before cutting and/or removing the paddle if necessary.

SWEET PICKLE BREAD

You can smell the typically British pickle in this bread, glorious with thick butter, hunks of Cheddar and extra pickle, and maybe salad on the side or cut-up apple. It brings the pub atmosphere home to the kitchen so keep the beer on ice, ready.

225 g/8 oz/1½ cups
(250 g/9 oz/1¾ cups)
soft grain strong white
bread flour

225 g/8 oz/1½ cups
(250 g/9 oz/1¾ cups)
country grain strong
brown bread flour

275 ml/10 fl oz/1¼ cups
(300 ml/11 fl oz/1⅜ cups)
water

2 tbsp (2¼ tbsp) oil

5 tbsp (6 tbsp) sweet
piccalilli

1½ tsp (1¾ tsp) salt

2 tsp (2½ tsp) caster sugar

1 tbsp (1¼ tbsp) dried
skimmed milk powder or
granules

1¼ tsp (1½ tsp) instant or
fast-acting dried yeast

glaze to taste (see
page 19)

Thoroughly mix together the two flours. Pour the water into the breadmaker bucket, then add the oil and piccalilli and half the mixed flours. Sprinkle with the salt, sugar and dried milk. Cover with the remaining flour mix and mound the yeast into the centre. Fit the bucket into the breadmaker and set to the programme recommended in the manual (usually basic white or No 1). When ready, carefully shake the loaf out of the bucket on to a wire cooling rack and stand the right way up. If liked, brush with the selected glaze. Leave the loaf for at least an hour before cutting and/or removing the paddle if necessary.

STILTON AND PORT BREAD

A select bread for ladies who lunch and gentlemen who make after-dinner speeches. A brown-crusted loaf with a pronounced flavour, pale beige interior and smooth texture. It slices easily and is appropriate with cheeses at the end of a meal or used for assorted sandwiches.

275 ml/10 fl oz/1¼ cups (300 ml/11 fl oz/1⅜ cups) water less 4 tbsp (5 tbsp)

4 tbsp (5 tbsp) port

100 g/3½ oz/1 cup (125 g/4 oz/1¼ cups) crumbled Stilton cheese

1 tbsp (1¼ tbsp) oil

450 g/16 oz/3 cups (500 g/17½ oz/3½ cups) strong white bread flour

1 tsp (1¼ tsp) salt

2 tsp (2½ tsp) caster sugar

1¼ tsp (1½ tsp) instant or fast-acting dried yeast

glaze to taste (see page 19)

Pour the water and port into the breadmaker bucket, then add the cheese, oil and half the flour. Sprinkle with the salt and sugar. Cover with the remaining flour and mound the yeast into the centre. Fit the bucket into the breadmaker and set to the programme recommended in the manual (usually basic white or No 1). When ready, carefully shake the loaf out of the bucket on to a wire cooling rack and stand the right way up. If liked, brush with the selected glaze. Leave the loaf for at least an hour before cutting and/or removing the paddle if necessary.

CHEDDAR CHEESE AND PALE ALE BREAD

A cheese bread that is a meal on its own with salad or eggs. The strength of its flavour will depend on the cheese, so I would suggest choosing one marked mature.

250 ml/9 fl oz/1⅛ cups pale ale or lager

25 ml/1 fl oz/⅛ cup water

1 tbsp oil

450 g/16 oz/3 cups soft grain strong white bread flour

100 g/3½ oz/1 cup grated Cheddar cheese

1½ tsp salt

2 tsp caster sugar

2 tbsp skimmed dried milk powder or granules

¾ tsp instant or fast-acting dried yeast

glaze to taste (see page 19)

Pour the ale or lager and water into the breadmaker bucket, then add the oil and half the flour. Sprinkle with the cheese, salt, sugar and dried milk. Cover with the remaining flour and mound the yeast into the centre. Fit the bucket into the breadmaker and set to the programme recommended in the manual (usually basic white or No 1). When ready, carefully shake the loaf out of the bucket on to a wire cooling rack and stand the right way up. If liked, brush with the selected glaze. Leave the loaf for at least an hour before cutting and/or removing the paddle if necessary.

CARROT AND CORIANDER BREAD

The elusive taste of carrot and the more forceful coriander make their own colourful contribution to a honey-gold loaf in what has become one of Britain's top-selling flavour combos. It's an adaptable bread and goes with almost anything savoury.

275 ml/10 fl oz/1¼ cups
(300 ml/11 fl oz/1⅜ cups)
organic carrot juice

2 tbsp oil

450 g/16 oz/3 cups
(500 g/17½ oz/3½ cups)
strong white bread flour

2 tsp (2¼ tsp) salt

4 tbsp (4½ tbsp) dried
coriander leaf

1 tbsp (1¼ tbsp) dried
skimmed milk powder or
granules

1½ tsp (1¾ tsp) instant or
fast-acting dried yeast

glaze to taste (see
page 19)

Pour the carrot juice into the breadmaker bucket, then add the oil and half the flour. Sprinkle with the salt, coriander and dried milk. Cover with the remaining flour and mound the yeast into the centre. Fit the bucket into the breadmaker and set to the programme recommended in the manual (usually basic white or No 1). When ready, carefully shake the loaf out of the bucket on to a wire cooling rack and stand the right way up. If liked, brush with the selected glaze. Leave the loaf for at least an hour before cutting and/or removing the paddle if necessary.

FRUIT AND NUT MUESLI BREAD

A nutritious breakfast bread with plenty of body to keep you going. It's brown and healthy and enjoyable with bananas, apple purée and berry fruits topped with yoghurt, or just fruit yoghurt by itself.

375 ml/13 fl oz/1⅝ cups water

2 tbsp oil

450 g/16 oz/3 cups strong brown (wholemeal) bread flour

1½ tsp salt

1 tbsp light brown soft sugar

2 tbsp skimmed dried milk powder or granules

50 g/2 oz/½ cup Swiss-style muesli with fruit and nuts

2 tsp instant or fast-acting dried yeast

glaze to taste (see page 19)

Pour the water into the breadmaker bucket, then add the oil and half the flour. Sprinkle with the salt, sugar, dried milk and muesli. Cover with the remaining flour and mound the yeast into the centre. Fit the bucket into the breadmaker and set to the programme recommended in the manual (usually wholemeal). When ready, carefully shake the loaf out of the bucket on to a wire cooling rack and stand the right way up. If liked, brush with the selected glaze. Leave the loaf for at least an hour before cutting and/or removing the paddle if necessary.

MEXICAN SPICED BREAD

A sassy bread, well-suited to guacamole, red bean salads, refried beans or chilli con carne. You can also eat the bread toasted or fried in oil with a vegetable salad for a quick snack.

275 ml/10 fl oz/1¼ cups (300 ml/11 fl oz/1⅜ cups) water

2 tbsp (2¼ tbsp) oil

450 g/16 oz/3 cups (500 g/17½ oz/3½ cups) soft grain strong white bread flour

2 tsp (2¼ tsp) salt

2 tsp (2¼ tsp) caster sugar

1 tbsp (1¼ tbsp) skimmed dried milk powder or granules

2 tbsp (2½ tbsp) Schwartz Tex-Mex spice

1 tsp (1¼ tsp) instant or fast-acting dried yeast

glaze to taste (see page 19)

Pour the water into the breadmaker bucket, then add the oil and half the flour. Sprinkle with the salt, sugar, milk and spice. Cover with the remaining flour and mound the yeast into the centre. Fit the bucket into the breadmaker and set to the programme recommended in the manual (usually basic white or No 1). When ready, carefully shake the loaf out of the bucket on to a wire cooling rack and stand the right way up. If liked, brush with the selected glaze. Leave the loaf for at least an hour before cutting and/or removing the paddle if necessary.

CRUNCHY PEANUT BUTTER BREAD

What can one say about a high-rise loaf flavoured with peanut butter? It's a stunner, predictably succulent when it's buttered and spread with Marmite. Or use it as a base for cheese on toast. All sound stuff with child appeal.

300 ml/11 fl oz/1⅜ cups water

3 tbsp crunchy peanut butter

1 tbsp oil

450 g/16 oz/3 cups soft grain strong white bread flour

1½ tsp salt

2 tsp caster sugar

2 tbsp dried skimmed milk powder or granules

1¼ tsp instant or fast-acting dried yeast

glaze to taste (see page 19)

Pour the water into the breadmaker bucket, then add the peanut butter, oil and half the flour. Sprinkle with the salt, sugar and dried milk. Cover with the remaining flour and mound the yeast into the centre. Fit the bucket into the breadmaker and set to the programme recommended in the manual (usually basic white or No 1). When ready, carefully shake the loaf out of the bucket on to a wire cooling rack and stand the right way up. If liked, brush with the selected glaze. Leave the loaf for at least an hour before cutting and/or removing the paddle if necessary.

SUNDRIED TOMATO AND RED PEPPER BREAD

A cheerful and assertive bread, have this aromatic loaf on tap for entertaining, especially if the food includes tapas.

275 ml/10 fl oz/1¼ cups (300 ml/11 fl oz/1⅜ cups) water

2 tbsp (2½ tbsp) olive oil

450 g/16 oz/3 cups (500 g/17½ oz/3½ cups) soft grain strong white bread flour

2 tsp (2¼ tsp) garlic salt

2 tsp (2½ tsp) caster sugar

2 tbsp (2½ tbsp) dried skimmed milk powder or granules

25 g/1 oz/½ cup (40 g/1½ oz/¾ cup) Chalice ready-to-eat sundried tomatoes, coarsely chopped

25 g/1 oz/½ cup (40 g/1½ oz/¾ cup) coarsely chopped red pepper

1¼ tsp (1½ tsp) instant or fast-acting dried yeast

glaze to taste (see page 19)

Pour the water into the breadmaker bucket, then add the oil and half the flour. Sprinkle with the salt, sugar, dried milk, tomatoes and peppers. Cover with the remaining flour and mound the yeast into the centre. Fit the bucket into the breadmaker and set to the programme recommended in the manual (usually basic white or No 1). When ready, carefully shake the loaf out of the bucket on to a wire cooling rack and stand the right way up. If liked, brush with the selected glaze. Leave the loaf for at least an hour before cutting and/or removing the paddle if necessary.

tea-time breads

MILK AND HONEY LOAF

Just a lovely, lovely bread and at its best when eaten with unsalted butter and raspberry jam.

3 tbsp thick honey

275 ml/10 fl oz/1¼ cups skimmed milk

2 tbsp melted butter

450 g/16 oz/3 cups strong white bread flour

1½ tsp salt

1½ tsp instant or fast-acting dried yeast

glaze to taste (see page 19)

Spoon the honey into the breadmaker bucket, then add the milk, melted butter and half the flour. Sprinkle with the salt. Cover with the remaining flour and mound the yeast into the centre. Fit the bucket into the breadmaker and set to the programme recommended in the manual (usually basic white or No 1). When ready, carefully shake the loaf out of the bucket on to a wire cooling rack and stand the right way up. If liked, brush with the selected glaze. Leave the loaf for at least an hour before cutting and/or removing the paddle if necessary.

FRUITED BUN LOAF

An exemplary semi-sweet fruited bread with a touch of spice and a hint of orange. It will do credit to any breadmaker and there's nothing more delicious for the tea table.

275 ml/10 fl oz/1¼ cups (300 ml/11 fl oz/1⅜ cups) water

1 tbsp (1¼ tbsp) oil

450 g/16 oz/3 cups (500 g/17½ oz/3½ cups) strong white bread flour

2 tsp (2½ tsp) mixed spice

1–2 tsp grated orange zest

1½ tsp (1¾ tsp) salt

2 tbsp (2½ tbsp) soft brown sugar

175 g/6 oz/1⅛ cups (200 g/7 oz/1¼ cups) luxury dried mixed fruit

1 tbsp (1¼ tbsp) dried skimmed milk powder or granules

1½ tsp (1¾ tsp) instant or fast-acting dried yeast

glaze to taste (see page 19)

Pour the water into the breadmaker bucket, then add the oil and half the flour. Sprinkle with the spice, orange zest, salt, sugar, dried fruit and milk. Cover with the remaining flour and mound the yeast into the centre. Fit the bucket into the breadmaker and set to the programme recommended in the manual (usually basic white or No 1). When ready, carefully shake the loaf out of the bucket on to a wire cooling rack and stand the right way up. If liked, brush with the selected glaze. Leave the loaf for an hour before cutting and/or removing the paddle if necessary.

FRUITED CURRANT LOAF

Prepare and bake exactly as for Fruited Bun Loaf, but use currants instead of dried mixed fruit.

SAFFRON AND CARDAMOM LOAF

The costly saffron is from the East and so is the cardamom, a much-loved spice in Scandinavia and Finland especially and widely used in Near and Far Eastern cooking. Put the two together and the perfume is magical, bread a kind of pale gold mystery with a feathery texture. Because it is only faintly sweet, it can be eaten with savoury foods and is particularly acceptable with Indian curries. The ground cardamom is available from Indian food shops.

1 sachet Schwartz saffron strands

1 tbsp boiling water

275 ml/10 fl oz/1¼ cups (300 ml/11 fl oz/1⅜ cups) cold water less 1 tbsp (4 tsp)

1 tbsp (1¼ tbsp) oil

450 g/16 oz/3 cups (500 g/17½ oz/3½ cups) strong white bread flour

1½ tsp (1¾ tsp) salt

2 tsp (2½ tsp) caster sugar

1 tbsp (4 tsp) ground cardamom

1¼ tsp (1½ tsp) instant or fast-acting dried yeast

glaze to taste (see page 19)

Soak the saffron in a small cup with the boiling water until cool. Pour with the cold water into the breadmaker bucket, then add the oil and half the flour. Sprinkle with the salt, sugar and cardamom. Cover with the remaining flour and mound the yeast into the centre. Fit the bucket into the breadmaker and set to the programme recommended in the manual (usually basic white or No 1). When ready, carefully shake the loaf out of the bucket on to a wire cooling rack and stand the right way up. If liked, brush with the selected glaze. Leave the loaf for at least an hour before cutting and/or removing the paddle if necessary.

MALT LOAF

Sticky and fruity as it should be, yet light and moist at the same time, this luscious dark bread is a prize specimen and can be eaten on its own as cake or sliced and buttered. Everyone will want some!

450 g/16 oz/3 cups soft grain strong white bread flour

1 tsp mixed spice

225 ml/8 fl oz/1 cup water

2 tbsp oil

3 tbsp malt extract

2 tbsp black treacle

1½ tsp salt

1¼ tsp instant or fast-acting dried yeast

150 g/3½ oz/⅔ cup ready-washed raisins

glaze to taste (see page 19)

Mix together the flour and spice. Pour the water into the breadmaker bucket, then add the oil, malt extract, treacle and half the flour mixture. Sprinkle with the salt. Cover with the remaining flour mix and mound the yeast into the centre. Fit the bucket into the breadmaker and set to the programme recommended in the manual (either special if the machine has this setting or basic white or No 1). Add the sultanas according to the manual's instructions, usually at the beginning or the middle of the second kneading or when the machine bleeps. When ready, carefully shake the loaf out of the bucket on to a wire cooling rack and stand the right way up. If liked, brush with the selected glaze. Leave the loaf for at least an hour before cutting and/or removing the paddle if necessary.

APRICOT AND ORANGE FLOWER WATER LOAF

Orange flower water, with its intangible fragrance reminiscent of eau de cologne, was once sold only in pharmacies and had to be ordered in advance, appearing in brown medicine bottles with corks. Now its stocked by leading supermarket chains as well as oriental food shops. When added to fruit salads and compôtes as well as bread, buns, biscuits and cakes, it leaves an exquisite, haunting after-taste, much favoured by cooks in eastern countries. Included in the bread with apricot jam, a little almond essence and orange zest for company, it makes a superior and lightly sweetened loaf and is a masterstroke in bread and butter pudding.

275 ml/10 fl oz/1¼ cups (300 ml/11 fl oz/1⅜ cups) water less 3 tbsp (4 tbsp)

3 tbsp (4 tbsp) orange flower water

1 tbsp (1¼ tbsp) oil

450 g/16 oz/3 cups (500 g/17½ oz/3½ cups) strong white bread flour

1½ tsp (1¾ tsp) salt

4 tbsp (4½ tbsp) apricot jam

2 tsp (2½ tsp) grated orange zest

1¼ tsp (1½ tsp) instant or fast-acting dried yeast

glaze to taste (see page 19)

Pour the water into the breadmaker bucket, then add the orange flower water, oil and half the flour. Sprinkle with the salt, then add the apricot jam and orange zest. Cover with the remaining flour and mound the yeast into the centre. Fit the bucket into the breadmaker and set to the programme recommended in the manual (usually basic white or No 1). When ready, carefully shake the loaf out of the bucket on to a wire cooling rack and stand the right way up. If liked, brush with the selected glaze. Leave the loaf for at least an hour before cutting and/or removing the paddle if necessary.

COCONUT ICE LOAF

Light, fluffy, smooth and soft, this golden-crusted loaf will delight everyone who loves coconut. It goes well with Thai and Malaysian food and is a novelty tea bread with lemon or orange curd or even thick chocolate spread. To turn into smart canapé bases, cut the loaf into long slices, stamp out smallish rounds with a biscuit cutter and fry in a little corn or groundnut oil until golden on both sides. Drain, cool and use.

300 ml/11 fl oz/1⅜ cups skimmed milk

1 tbsp oil

1 tsp vanilla essence

450 g/16 oz/3 cups strong white bread flour

1½ tsp salt

3 tbsp icing sugar

50 g/2 oz/⅔ cup desiccated coconut

1½ tsp instant or fast-acting dried yeast

glaze to taste (see page 19)

Pour the milk into the breadmaker bucket, then add the oil, vanilla and half the flour. Sprinkle with the salt, sugar and coconut. Cover with the remaining flour and mound the yeast into the centre. Fit the bucket into the breadmaker and set to the programme recommended in the manual (usually basic white or No 1). When ready, carefully shake the loaf out of the bucket on to a wire cooling rack and stand the right way up. If liked, brush with the selected glaze. Leave the loaf for at least an hour before cutting and/or removing the paddle if necessary.

MOCHA LOAF

An irresistible cross between a loaf and a cake, the coffee and chocolate intertwined in the background, the sweetness light. It makes a kind of French-style breakfast bread, a chocolate croissant substitute, and may be eaten plain or buttered and topped with soft cream cheese.

300 ml/11 fl oz/1⅜ cups water

1 tbsp oil

450 g/16 oz/3 cups strong white bread flour, less 3 tbsp

3 tbsp cocoa powder, sifted

2 tbsp instant coffee granules

1½ tsp salt

3 tbsp light brown soft sugar

1 tbsp chocolate hazelnut spread

2 tbsp skimmed dried milk powder or granules

1½ tsp instant or fast-acting dried yeast

glaze to taste (see page 19)

Pour the water into the breadmaker bucket, then add the oil and half the flour. Sprinkle with the cocoa powder, coffee, salt and sugar. Add the chocolate spread and dried milk. Cover with the remaining flour and mound the yeast into the centre. Fit the bucket into the breadmaker and set to the programme recommended in the manual (either sweet if the machine has this setting or basic white or No 1). When ready, carefully shake the loaf out of the bucket on to a wire cooling rack and stand the right way up. If liked, brush with the selected glaze. Leave the loaf for at least an hour before cutting and/or removing the paddle if necessary.

GOOSEBERRY AND ELDERFLOWER LOAF

The marriage made in heaven of gooseberry and elderflower never dates and this beautiful-tasting loaf bears all the hallmarks of a British summer and the tranquil calm of the countryside.

275 ml/10 fl oz/1¼ cups (300 ml/11 fl oz/1⅜ cups) water

2 tbsp (2½ tbsp) melted unsalted butter

450 g/16 oz/3 cups (500 g/17½ oz/3½ cups) strong white bread flour

1½ tsp (1¾ tsp) salt

2 tbsp (2½ tbsp) skimmed dried milk powder or granules

4 tbsp (4½ tbsp) gooseberry jam

3 tbsp (3½ tbsp) elderflower cordial

1½ tsp (1¾ tsp) instant or fast-acting dried yeast

glaze to taste (see page 19)

Pour the water into the breadmaker bucket, then add the butter and half the flour. Sprinkle with the salt and dried milk and add the jam and cordial. Cover with the remaining flour and mound the yeast into the centre. Fit the bucket into the breadmaker and set to the programme recommended in the manual (usually basic white or No 1). When ready, carefully shake the loaf out of the bucket on to a wire cooling rack and stand the right way up. If liked, brush with the selected glaze. Leave the loaf for at least an hour before cutting and/or removing the paddle if necessary.

MILK LOAF

A childhood loaf, the simplest pleasure in some ways, and also one that made teatime with clotted cream and strawberry jam such a sumptuous feast. Revive it for old time's sake.

275 ml/10 fl oz/1¼ cups
(300 ml/11 fl oz/1⅜ cups)
skimmed milk

1 tbsp (1¼ tbsp) oil or
melted butter

450 g/16 oz/3 cups
(500 g/17½ oz/3½ cups)
strong white bread flour

1½ tsp (1¾ tsp) salt

2 tsp (2¼ tsp) caster sugar

1¼ tsp (1½ tsp) instant or
fast-acting dried yeast

glaze to taste (see
page 19)

Pour the milk into the breadmaker, add the oil or melted butter and half the flour. Sprinkle with the salt and sugar, then cover with the remaining flour and mound the yeast into the centre. Fit the bucket into the breadmaker and set to the programme recommended in the manual (usually basic white or No 1). When ready, carefully shake the loaf out of the bucket on to a wire cooling rack and stand the right way up. If liked, brush with the selected glaze. Leave the loaf for at least an hour before cutting and/or removing the paddle if necessary.

gluten-free breads

GLUTEN-FREE BREADS

Allergies or sensitivities to certain foods are not uncommon and coeliacs are a group of people with an allergy to gluten found in wheat, resulting in a medical condition known as coeliac disease. Sufferers are unable to cope with anything containing wheat flour and may also be sensitive to similar proteins contained in rye, barley and sometimes oats. About one person in every three hundred of the population is a coeliac, though often undiagnosed, and the Coeliac Society, which offers a back-up service, recipe book and dictionary of permitted or safe foods, has 40,000 registered members. Diet control is a key factor in helping coeliacs overcome some of their distressing and debilitating symptoms and a number of dietary specialists have come into the marketplace with gluten-free flour and baking mixes, some available on prescription, providing coeliacs with an opportunity to bake their own crusty and tasty bread with comparative ease and live like the rest of us. Juvela, part of SHS International, has been a tower of strength to me in developing this and the next chapter of gluten-free breads exclusively for breadmakers, and other organisations have also provided educational material and trial products. I thank them all.

NOTES
◆ All the loaves in this section weigh in the region of 600–650 g or 20–23 oz, near enough 1¼–1½ lb.
◆ Where an asterisk (*) is shown against an ingredient, check with the Coeliac Society's dictionary to make sure it is gluten-free.
◆ The recipes in this chapter use the wholemeal programme. It takes longer, but this setting is beneficial when making gluten-free bread with the Juvela mix.

BASIC GLUTEN-FREE WHITE LOAF

300 ml/11 fl oz/1⅜ cups water

1 tbsp oil

350 g/12 oz/2¾ cups Juvela gluten-free mix

½ tsp salt

1 tsp yeast (taken from the pack supplied with the Juvela gluten-free mix)

glaze to taste (see page 19)

Pour the water into the breadmaker bucket, then add the oil and half the mix. Sprinkle with the salt. Cover with the remaining mix and mound the yeast into the centre. Fit the bucket into the breadmaker and set to the wholewheat programme. When ready, carefully shake the loaf out of the bucket on to a wire cooling rack and stand the right way up. If liked, brush with the selected glaze. Leave the loaf for at least an hour before cutting and/or removing the paddle if necessary.

BASIC GLUTEN-FREE FIBRE LOAF

Prepare and bake exactly as for Basic Gluten-free White Loaf, but use Juvela gluten-free fibre mix and add an extra 1½ tbsp water to the original amount.

CAJUN SPICED BREAD

A loaf steaming in from Mississippi with all the character and spiciness of North America's Deep South. It's totally at home with barbecued food, grilled sausages, fried fish, juicy omelettes and the rice-laden jambalaya brimming with chicken and okra. A joy.

300 ml/11 fl oz/1⅜ cups water plus 1½ tbsp

1 tbsp oil

350 g/12 oz/2¾ cups Juvela gluten-free fibre mix

½ tsp salt

1½ tsp Schwartz Cajun Grill and Sizzle mix or 2 tsp Cajun seasoning

1 tsp yeast (taken from the pack supplied with the Julvela gluten-free fibre mix)

glaze to taste (see page 19)

Pour the water into the breadmaker bucket, then add the oil and half the mix. Sprinkle with the salt and the Cajun seasoning. Cover with the remaining mix and mound the yeast into the centre. Fit the bucket into the breadmaker and set to the wholewheat programme. When ready, carefully shake the loaf out of the bucket on to a wire cooling rack and stand the right way up. If liked, brush with the selected glaze. Leave the loaf for at least an hour before cutting and/or removing the paddle if necessary.

SPICY ITALIAN TOMATO BREAD

Slice this one fairly thickly, cover each slice with Mozzarella cheese, toast under the grill and there you have it – instant Pizza, as good as anything you can buy or eat in a restaurant. And you can also add topping extras like olives, capers, sliced fried mushrooms, peperoni sausage, ham, pineapple and red pepper strips or whatever else takes your fancy. Great for parties and a fast feast.

300 ml/11 fl oz/1⅜ cups water plus 1½ tbsp

1 tbsp olive oil

1 tbsp tomato ketchup*

350 g/12 oz/2¾ cups Juvela gluten-free fibre mix

2 tbsp dried basil

½ tsp salt

1 tsp yeast (taken from the pack supplied with the Juvela gluten-free fibre mix)

glaze to taste (see page 19)

Pour the water into the breadmaker bucket, then add the oil, ketchup, and half the mix. Sprinkle with the basil and salt. Cover with the remaining mix and mound the yeast into the centre. Fit the bucket into the breadmaker and set to the wholewheat programme. When ready, carefully shake the loaf out of the bucket on to a wire cooling rack and stand the right way up. If liked, brush with the selected glaze. Leave the loaf for at least an hour before cutting and/or removing the paddle if necessary.

MAYONNAISE BREAD

An elegant and creamy white bread with a delicate flavour and almost cake-like texture, the mayonnaise eliminating the need for oil. It's great with eggs, hard-boiled especially, in sarnies with cress and tomato, and also makes an appropriate accompaniment to smoked and fresh salmon, fresh crab or smoked mackerel and prawn cocktail.

350 ml/12 fl oz/1½ cups water

2 tbsp best-quality mayonnaise*

350 g/12 oz/2¾ cups Juvela gluten-free mix

½ tsp salt

1 tsp yeast (taken from the pack supplied with the Juvela gluten-free mix)

glaze to taste (see page 19)

Pour the water into the breadmaker bucket, then add the mayonnaise and half the mix. Sprinkle with the salt. Cover with the remaining mix and mound the yeast into the centre. Fit the bucket into the breadmaker and set to the wholewheat programme. When ready, carefully shake the loaf out of the bucket on to a wire cooling rack and stand the right way up. If liked, brush with the selected glaze. Leave the loaf for at least an hour before cutting and/or removing the paddle if necessary.

SMOKY SEED BREAD

The bread is strikingly dominant, wonderful with strong cheeses, salami and smoked meats. It also takes well to being toasted and buttered and eaten with a coarse liver or game pâté.

2 tbsp white hulled sesame seeds

2 tsp yellow mustard seeds

2 tsp cumin seeds

2 tbsp sesame oil

300 ml/11 fl oz/1⅜ cups water

350 g/12 oz/2¾ cups Juvela gluten-free mix

½ tsp salt

1 tsp yeast (taken from the pack supplied with the Juvela gluten-free mix)

glaze to taste (see page 19)

Fry the three seeds in the sesame oil gently for 3 minutes, stirring all the time. Pour the water into the breadmaker bucket, then the fried seeds and their oil and half the mix. Sprinkle with the salt. Cover with the remaining mix and mound the yeast into the centre. Fit the bucket into the breadmaker and set to the wholewheat programme. When ready, carefully shake the loaf out of the bucket on to a wire cooling rack and stand the right way up. If liked, brush with the selected glaze. Leave the loaf for at least an hour before cutting and/or removing the paddle if necessary.

TOMATO, WORCESTERSHIRE AND TABASCO SAUCE BREAD

Orange-toned and spiky to the taste buds, the liquid in the bread is virtually a home-blended tomato juice cocktail, the result being a wonderfully peppy loaf for bacon or ham sandwiches, to have with cheese and crisp celery at the end of a meal, to slice and toast and drizzle while hot with virgin olive oil and a dusting of garlic salt or roasted and squashed garlic.

140 g/5 oz/⅝ cup tubed or canned tomato purée*

warm water

4 tsp Worcestershire sauce

8 drops of Tabasco sauce

350 g/12 oz/2¾ cups Juvela gluten-free mix

½ tsp celery salt

1 tsp yeast (taken from the pack supplied with the Juvela gluten-free mix)

glaze to taste (see page 19)

Spoon tomato purée into a measuring jug and blend smoothly with a little warm water. Make up to 275 ml/10 fl oz/1¼ cups with extra water, then add the Worcestershire and Tabasco sauces. Pour into the breadmaker bucket and add half the mix. Sprinkle with the celery salt. Cover with the remaining mix and mound the yeast into the centre. Fit the bucket into the breadmaker and set to the wholewheat programme. When ready, carefully shake the loaf out of the bucket on to a wire cooling rack and stand the right way up. If liked, brush with the selected glaze. Leave the loaf for at least an hour before cutting and/or removing the paddle if necessary.

FRAGRANT CHINESE SPICED BREAD

A dignified and delicately aromatic bread, designed to accompany stir-fries and roast duck.

300 ml/11 fl oz/1⅜ cups water plus 1½ tbsp

1 tbsp rice or groundnut oil

2 tbsp reduced-salt soy sauce*

2 tsp Chinese five-spice paste*

350 g/12 oz/2¾ cups Juvela gluten-free fibre mix

¼ tsp salt

1 tsp yeast (taken from the pack supplied with the Julvela gluten-free fibre mix)

glaze to taste (see page 19)

Pour the water into the breadmaker bucket. Combine the oil with the soy sauce and five-spice paste, then add to the water with half the mix. Sprinkle with the salt. Cover with the remaining mix and mound the yeast into the centre. Fit the bucket into the breadmaker and set to the wholewheat programme. When ready, carefully shake the loaf out of the bucket on to a wire cooling rack and stand the right way up. If liked, brush with the selected glaze. Leave the loaf for at least an hour before cutting and/or removing the paddle if necessary.

ENGLISH MUSTARD BREAD

A dream, this one, with the most fabulous flavour and beautiful texture. It goes with anything from cold roast beef and salad to fried eggs and meatballs.

300 ml/11 fl oz/1⅜ cups water

1 tbsp oil

4 tsp prepared English mustard*

350 g/12 oz/2¾ cups Juvela gluten-free mix

½ tsp salt

1 tsp yeast (taken from the pack supplied with the Juvela gluten-free mix)

glaze to taste (see page 19)

Pour the water into the breadmaker bucket, then add the oil, mustard and half the mix. Sprinkle with the salt. Cover with the remaining mix and mound the yeast into the centre. Fit the bucket into the breadmaker and set to the wholewheat programme. When ready, carefully shake the loaf out of the bucket on to a wire cooling rack and stand the right way up. If liked, brush with the selected glaze. Leave the loaf for at least an hour before cutting and/or removing the paddle if necessary.

CHUTNEY AND SULTANA BREAD

Perfect with cheese, especially mature Cheddar and Stilton and strong smellers from France, Germany and Denmark. Also comfortable with corned beef and roast chicken, barbecued foods and grilled gammon rashers.

300 ml/11 fl oz/1⅜ cups water plus 1½ tbsp

1 tbsp oil

350 g/12 oz/2¾ cups Juvela gluten-free fibre mix

½ tsp salt

3 tbsp fruit chutney*, chopped if necessary

3 tbsp ready-washed sultanas

1 tsp yeast (taken from the pack supplied with the Juvela gluten-free fibre mix)

glaze to taste (see page 19)

Pour the water into the breadmaker bucket, then add the oil and half the mix. Sprinkle with the salt, chutney and sultanas. Cover with the remaining mix and mound the yeast into the centre. Fit the bucket into the breadmaker and set to the wholewheat programme. When ready, carefully shake the loaf out of the bucket on to a wire cooling rack and stand the right way up. If liked, brush with the selected glaze. Leave the loaf for at least an hour before cutting and/or removing the paddle if necessary.

JAPANESE BREAD

A novelty bread to have with clear noodle soup, sushi or any other oriental food from Thai to Chinese. The texture is smooth, the taste unusual and the colour honey gold. Wasabi is Japanese horseradish.

2 tbsp soy sauce*

water

1 tbsp oil

350 g/12 oz/2¾ cups Juvela gluten-free mix

¼ tsp salt

2 tsp Japanese wasabi powder*

1 tsp yeast (taken from the pack supplied with the Julvela gluten-free mix)

glaze to taste (see page 19)

Make up the soy sauce to 300 ml/11 fl oz/1⅜ cups with water, then pour into the breadmaker bucket. Add the oil and half the mix. Sprinkle with the salt and wasabi powder. Cover with the remaining mix and mound the yeast into the centre. Fit the bucket into the breadmaker and set to the wholewheat programme. When ready, carefully shake the loaf out of the bucket on to a wire cooling rack and stand the right way up. If liked, brush with the selected glaze. Leave the loaf for at least an hour before cutting and/or removing the paddle if necessary.

RASPBERRY AND CINNAMON LOAF

A teatime treat. The flavour is reminiscent of Austria's famous Linzertorte, a world class classic cake from the town of Linz. Slice it and spread with butter or margarine and extra raspberry jam.

300 ml/11 fl oz/1⅜ cups water plus 1½ tbsp

1 tbsp oil

350 g/12 oz/2¾ cups Juvela gluten-free fibre mix

½ tsp salt

2 tsp ground cinnamon

4 tbsp raspberry jam

1 tsp yeast (taken from the pack supplied with the Juvela gluten-free fibre mix)

glaze to taste (see page 19)

Pour the water into the breadmaker bucket, then add the oil and half the mix. Sprinkle with the salt and cinnamon. Add the raspberry jam in dollops over the mix. Cover with the remaining mix and mound the yeast into the centre. Fit the bucket into the breadmaker and set to the wholewheat programme. When ready, carefully shake the loaf out of the bucket on to a wire cooling rack and stand the right way up. If liked, brush with the selected glaze. Leave the loaf for at least an hour before cutting and/or removing the paddle if necessary.

BUTTERED HONEY LOAF WITH NUTMEG

Bread with a heart of gold!

3 tbsp clear dark honey

2 tbsp hot water

water at room temperature

1½ tbsp melted unsalted butter

350 g/12 oz/2¾ cups Juvela gluten-free mix

½ tsp salt

⅛ tsp grated nutmeg

1 tsp yeast (taken from the pack supplied with the Juvela gluten-free mix)

glaze to taste (see page 19)

Mix the honey with the hot water, then add sufficient room temperature water to make up to 300 ml/11 fl oz/1⅜ cups. Pour the mixture into the breadmaker bucket, then add the butter and half the mix. Sprinkle with the salt and nutmeg. Cover with the remaining mix and mound the yeast into the centre. Fit the bucket into the breadmaker and set to the wholewheat programme. When ready, carefully shake the loaf out of the bucket on to a wire cooling rack and stand the right way up. If liked, brush with the selected glaze. Leave the loaf for at least an hour before cutting and/or removing the paddle if necessary.

CINNAMON AND RAISIN LOAF

A hint of spice enlivens the bread and the raisins add their own brand of delicate sweetness.

300 ml/11 fl oz/1⅜ cups water plus 1½ tbsp

1 tbsp oil

350 g/12 oz/2¾ cups Juvela gluten-free fibre mix

½ tsp salt

1 tsp ground cinnamon

6 tbsp ready-washed raisins

1 tsp yeast (taken from the pack supplied with the Juvela gluten-free fibre mix)

glaze to taste (see page 19)

Pour the water into the breadmaker bucket, then add the oil and half the mix. Sprinkle with the salt, cinnamon and raisins. Cover with the remaining mix and mound the yeast into the centre. Fit the bucket into the breadmaker and set to the wholewheat programme. When ready, carefully shake the loaf out of the bucket on to a wire cooling rack and stand the right way up. If liked, brush with the selected glaze. Leave the loaf for at least an hour before cutting and/or removing the paddle if necessary.

CHOCOLATE HAZELNUT LOAF

An absolute winner, chocolate-coloured and with a subtle hint of hazelnuts coming through as you eat it. When freshly baked and sliced, and spread with Marscarpone you can hear the angels sing.

300 ml/11 fl oz/1⅜ cups water

1 tbsp oil

350 g/12 oz/2¾ cups Juvela gluten-free mix

½ tsp salt

3 tbsp chocolate hazelnut spread

1 tsp yeast (taken from the pack supplied with the Juvela gluten-free mix)

glaze to taste (see page 19)

Pour the water into the breadmaker bucket, then add the oil and half the mix. Sprinkle with the salt, then dollop in the spread. Cover with the remaining mix and mound the yeast into the centre. Fit the bucket into the breadmaker and set to the wholewheat programme. When ready, carefully shake the loaf out of the bucket on to a wire cooling rack and stand the right way up. If liked, brush with the selected glaze. Leave the loaf for at least an hour before cutting and/or removing the paddle if necessary.

CITRUS LOAF

For anyone into oranges and lemons, this has to be the absolute best!

300 ml/11 fl oz/1⅜ cups water

1 tbsp oil

350 g/12 oz/2¾ cups Juvela gluten-free mix

½ tsp salt

2 tbsp fine-cut orange marmalade

1 tbsp buttery lemon curd

1 tsp yeast (taken from the pack supplied with the Juvela gluten-free mix)

glaze to taste (see page 19)

Pour the water into the breadmaker bucket, then add the oil and half the mix. Sprinkle with the salt, then dollop in the marmalade and lemon curd. Cover with the remaining mix and mound the yeast into the centre. Fit the bucket into the breadmaker and set to the wholewheat programme. When ready, carefully shake the loaf out of the bucket on to a wire cooling rack and stand the right way up. If liked, brush with the selected glaze. Leave the loaf for at least an hour before cutting and/or removing the paddle if necessary.

TREACLE AND PECAN LOAF

A forceful character to this one, 'Americanised' with hickory nuts, better known as pecans.

300 ml/11 fl oz/1⅜ cups water plus 1½ tbsp

1 tbsp oil

1 tbsp black treacle

350 g/12 oz/2¾ cups Juvela gluten-free fibre mix

½ tsp salt

4–5 tbsp pecan nuts, coarsely chopped

1 tsp yeast (taken from the pack supplied with the Juvela gluten-free fibre mix)

glaze to taste (see page 19)

Pour the water into the breadmaker bucket, then add the oil, treacle and half the mix. Sprinkle with the salt and chopped pecans. Cover with the remaining mix and mound the yeast into the centre. Fit the bucket into the breadmaker and set to the wholewheat programme. When ready, carefully shake the loaf out of the bucket on to a wire cooling rack and stand the right way up. If liked, brush with the selected glaze. Leave the loaf for at least an hour before cutting and/or removing the paddle if necessary.

dairy-free breads

DAIRY-FREE BREADS

Just as there are people unable to tolerate gluten, so there are also those who are sensitive to the lactose in dairy products made from cows' milk. This short section of assorted breads is for them.

MARMITE LOAF

Not too strong, just a gentle breath of Marmite coming through to make the bread interesting enough for Marmite enthusiasts. When cut and spread with peanut butter, it's the stuff that dreams are made of, likewise as a base for Welsh Rarebit. Because Marmite is, of itself, high in yeast, the amount of instant or fast-acting dried yeast has been reduced in the recipe. Without this adjustment, the bread would rise too much and then collapse.

3 tsp Marmite

1 tbsp hot water

275 ml/10 fl oz/1¼ cups cold water less 1 tbsp

2 tbsp oil

450 g/16 oz/3 cups soft grain strong white bread flour

½ tsp salt

1½ tsp caster sugar

½ tsp instant or fast-acting dried yeast

glaze to taste (see page 19)

Mix the Marmite with a little of the hot water, then pour into the breadmaker bucket with the cold water. Add the oil and half the flour. Sprinkle with the salt and sugar. Cover with the remaining flour and mound the yeast into the centre. Fit the bucket into the breadmaker and set to the programme recommended in the manual (usually basic white or No 1). When ready, carefully shake the loaf out of the bucket on to a wire cooling rack and stand the right way up. If liked, brush with the selected glaze. Leave the loaf for at least an hour before cutting and/or removing the paddle if necessary.

SPICY HOT BREAD

Aromatic and deep cream-coloured, keep this one for burgers, sausages and barbecues. You can also eat it with curries and tandoori chicken instead of Indian bread. Its texture is almost satiny.

2 tbsp Worcestershire sauce

1–2 tsp Tabasco sauce

3 tsp vegetarian stock powder

1 tbsp hot water

275 ml/10 fl oz/1¼ cups cold water less 1 tbsp

2 tbsp oil

450 g/16 oz/3 cups strong white bread flour

1¼ tsp salt

1½ tsp caster sugar

1½ tsp instant or fast-acting dried yeast

glaze to taste (see page 19)

Mix the first three ingredients smoothly together with the hot water, then add to the breadmaker bucket with the cold water. Add the oil and half the flour. Sprinkle with the salt and sugar. Cover with the remaining flour and mound the yeast into the centre. Fit the bucket into the breadmaker and set to the programme recommended in the manual (usually basic white or No 1). When ready, carefully shake the loaf out of the bucket on to a wire cooling rack and stand the right way up. If liked, brush with the selected glaze. Leave the loaf for at least an hour before cutting and/or removing the paddle if necessary.

POTATO AND DILL BREAD

When I first made the bread and tried a piece of it, I wrote 'fantastic' in my notes because the texture was soft and downy, the loaf well-shaped and the crust just right. When I went back a second time to double check, it was just as appetising and just as enjoyable and has remained in my family's good books ever since. The dried dill gives only a hint of herb, so if you prefer something more pronounced use rosemary or thyme or a mixture of dried herbs. The flour people at Allinson add caraway seeds so, if the taste appeals, include 1 tsp with the potatoes. The bread is companionable with smoked fish, eggs and vegetable soups.

275 ml/10 fl oz/1¼ cups rice milk

1 tbsp oil

450 g/16 oz/3 cups strong white bread flour

2 tsp salt

1½ tsp caster sugar

3 tsp Schwartz dried dill

125 g/4 oz/⅞ cup grated cooked potato, waxy and not floury

1¼ tsp instant or fast-acting dried yeast

glaze to taste (see page 19)

Pour the rice milk into the breadmaker bucket, then add the oil and half the flour. Sprinkle with the salt, sugar, dill and potato. Cover with the remaining flour and mound the yeast into the centre. Fit the bucket into the breadmaker and set to the programme recommended in the manual (usually basic white or No 1). When ready, carefully shake the loaf out of the bucket on to a wire cooling rack and stand the right way up. If liked, brush with the selected glaze. Leave the loaf for at least an hour before cutting and/or removing the paddle if necessary.

CARROT AND NUTMEG BREAD

An amber-coloured and light-textured loaf, spiced with nutmeg and mild enough to go with both sweet and savoury food. It behaves well, rises beautifully and is great stuff with mixed vegetables, curries and equally satisfying with other vegetarian stews and casseroles.

225 g/8 oz/1½ cups soft grain strong white bread flour

225 g/8 oz/1½ cups strong brown (wholemeal) flour

300 ml/11 fl oz/1⅜ cups organic carrot juice

2 tbsp oil

1¼ tsp salt

1 tsp caster sugar

1 tsp freshly grated nutmeg

1¼ tsp instant or fast-acting dried yeast

glaze to taste (see page 19)

Thoroughly mix together the two flours. Pour the carrot juice into the breadmaker bucket, then add the oil, then half the mixed flours. Sprinkle with the salt, sugar and nutmeg. Cover with the remaining flour mix and mound the yeast into the centre. Fit the bucket into the breadmaker and set to the programme recommended in the manual (usually basic white or No 1). When ready, carefully shake the loaf out of the bucket on to a wire cooling rack and stand the right way up. If liked, brush with the selected glaze. Leave the loaf for at least an hour before cutting and/or removing the paddle if necessary.

COCONUT AND ROSE WATER LOAF

The merest scent of rose comes through in this delicate bread which can be turned into puddings or eaten with margarine and jam or marmalade for breakfast or tea. It toasts beautifully.

275 ml/10 fl oz/1¼ cups coconut milk less 3 tbsp

3 tbsp rose water

2 tbsp oil

450 g/16 oz/3 cups strong white bread flour

1½ tsp salt

2 tbsp vanilla sugar

1½ tsp instant or fast-acting dried yeast

glaze to taste (see page 19)

Pour the coconut milk and rose water into the breadmaker bucket, then add the oil and half the flour. Sprinkle with the salt and vanilla sugar. Cover with the remaining flour and mound the yeast into the centre. Fit the bucket into the breadmaker and set to the programme recommended in the manual (sweet if the machine has this setting or basic white or No 1). When ready, carefully shake the loaf out of the bucket on to a wire cooling rack and stand the right way up. If liked, brush with the selected glaze. Leave the loaf for at least an hour before cutting and/or removing the paddle if necessary.

BEETROOT, ONION AND CARAWAY SEED LOAF

A touch of whimsy here with a savoury bread coloured deep rose pink and flavoured with onion and optional caraway. It's quite an eye opener and always draws attention to itself – just the thing to break the ice at a dinner party of strangers.

300 ml/11 fl oz/1⅜ cups organic beetroot juice

2 tbsp oil

450 g/16 oz/3 cups soft grain strong white bread flour

2 tsp onion salt

1 tsp caraway seeds (optional)

1¼ tsp instant or fast-acting dried yeast

glaze to taste (see page 19)

Pour the beetroot juice into the breadmaker bucket, then add the oil and half the flour. Sprinkle with the onion salt and caraway seeds, if using. Cover with the remaining flour and mound the yeast into the centre. Fit the bucket into the breadmaker and set to the programme recommended in the manual (usually basic white or No 1). When ready, carefully shake the loaf out of the bucket on to a wire cooling rack and stand the right way up. If liked, brush with the selected glaze. Leave the loaf for at least an hour before cutting and/or removing the paddle if necessary.

SUNDRIED RED PEPPER BREAD

A forthright bread with great individuality and dotted with sundried peppers. Try it with soups, olives in all colours and omelettes.

150 ml/5 fl oz/⅝ cup vegetable juice such as V8

water

1 tbsp olive oil

450 g/16 oz/3 cups strong white bread flour

1½ tsp salt

1 tbsp soft brown sugar

25 g/1 oz/½ cup ready-to-eat sundried peppers, scissor-snipped into small pieces

1¼ tsp instant or fast-acting dried yeast

glaze to taste (see page 19)

Make up the vegetable juice to 275 ml/10 fl oz/1¼ cups with water. Pour into the breadmaker bucket, then add the oil and half the flour. Sprinkle with the salt, sugar and peppers. Cover with the remaining flour and mound the yeast into the centre. Fit the bucket into the breadmaker and set to the programme recommended in the manual (usually basic white or No 1). When ready, carefully shake the loaf out of the bucket on to a wire cooling rack and stand the right way up. If liked, brush with the selected glaze. Leave the loaf for at least an hour before cutting and/or removing the paddle if necessary.

SMOKY CHINESE BREAD

The lapsong souchong tea and five-spice powder are happy teammates and work smoothly together to make a slightly sweet loaf with a subtle oriental taste. The bread shapes up superbly and would go with almost any Chinese meal or stir-fry.

275 ml/10 fl oz/1¼ cups cooled lapsang souchong tea

2 tbsp oil

450 g/16 oz/3 cups strong white bread flour

2 tsp five-spice powder

1¼ tsp salt

2 tbsp soft brown sugar caster sugar

1½ tsp instant or fast-acting dried yeast

glaze to taste (see page 19)

Strain the tea if made with leaves, then pour into the breadmaker bucket. Add the oil and half the flour. Sprinkle with the five-spice powder, salt and sugar. Cover with the remaining flour and mound the yeast into the centre. Fit the bucket into the breadmaker and set to the programme recommended in the manual (usually basic white or No 1). When ready, carefully shake the loaf out of the bucket on to a wire cooling rack and stand the right way up. If liked, brush with the selected glaze. Leave the loaf for at least an hour before cutting and/or removing the paddle if necessary.

BEER AND FRENCH MUSTARD BREAD

Using lager and Dijon mustard together, you get bread with a faint aftertaste of both and the slight crunch of the soft grain flour gives it added style. It's a country bread and looks it, earthy enough to go with sausages, cold meat pies and chicken, hard boiled eggs, roast vegetables and gutsy salads with strong Mediterranean flavours.

25 cl bottle/8 fl oz/1 cup lager

water

2 tbsp oil

4 tsp Dijon mustard

225 g/8 oz/1½ cups soft grain strong white bread flour

225 g/8 oz/1½ cups strong white bread flour

1¼ tsp salt

1½ tsp caster sugar

¾ tsp instant or fast-acting dried yeast

glaze to taste (see page 13)

Make up the lager to 300 ml/11 fl oz/1⅜ cups with water. Pour into the breadmaker bucket, then add the oil and mustard. Mix together the two flours and add half to the bucket. Sprinkle with the salt and sugar. Cover with the remaining flour mix and mound the yeast into the centre. Fit the bucket into the breadmaker and set to the programme recommended in the manual (usually basic white or No 1). When ready, carefully shake the loaf out of the bucket on to a wire cooling rack and stand the right way up. If liked, brush with the selected glaze. Leave the loaf for at least an hour before cutting and/or removing the paddle if necessary.

BEEFEATERS' BREAD WITH CONSOMME AND HORSERADISH

Made with consommé and grated horseradish, the bread is wholesome and savoury, densely textured, perfect for mopping up stew and casserole gravies. It's also a useful sandwich bread for foods like cold roast beef, tongue and ham off the bone.

300 ml/11 fl oz/1⅜ cups canned consommé, diluted according to can instructions if concentrated

2 tbsp oil

5 tsp hot horseradish, coarsely grated (bought in a jar or bottle)

450 g/16 oz/3 cups strong brown bread flour (wholemeal)

1 tsp salt

1½ tsp caster sugar

1¼ tsp instant or fast-acting dried yeast

glaze to taste (see page 19)

Pour the consommé into the breadmaker bucket, then add the oil, horseradish and half the flour. Sprinkle with the salt and sugar. Cover with the remaining flour and mound the yeast into the centre. Fit the bucket into the breadmaker and set to the programme recommended in the manual (usually wholemeal). When ready, carefully shake the loaf out of the bucket on to a wire cooling rack and stand the right way up. If liked, brush with the selected glaze. Leave the loaf for at least an hour before cutting and/or removing the paddle if necessary.

APPLE AND CINNAMON LOAF

A gently mellow loaf full of the sweet perfumes of autumn, well-risen and soft-textured. It has a fine shape and smooth crumb and is magnificent with apple butter, lemon or orange curd, chunky marmalade or thick heather honey.

275 ml/10 fl oz/1¼ cups apple juice

2 tbsp oil

450 g/16 oz/3 cups strong white bread flour

2 tsp cinnamon

1¼ tsp salt

1½ tsp caster sugar

1¼ tsp instant or fast-acting dried yeast

glaze to taste (see page 19)

Pour the apple juice into the breadmaker bucket, then add the oil and half the flour. Sprinkle with the cinnamon, salt and sugar. Cover with the remaining flour and mound the yeast into the centre. Fit the bucket into the breadmaker and set to the programme recommended in the manual (usually basic white or No 1). When ready, carefully shake the loaf out of the bucket on to a wire cooling rack and stand the right way up. If liked, brush with the selected glaze. Leave the loaf for at least an hour before cutting and/or removing the paddle if necessary.

BANANA CHIP BREAD

A fairly close-textured loaf that slices well and reasonably thinly. Because the banana flavour hovers in the background without dominating, the bread can be eaten with sweet or savoury foods and is outstanding with bacon and gammon steaks or, on the other side of the coin, with chocolate spread.

275 ml/10 fl oz/1¼ cups soy milk

1 tbsp oil

450 g/16 oz/3 cups strong white bread flour

1½ tsp salt

1 tsp caster sugar

1½ tsp instant or fast-acting dried yeast

125 g/4 oz/1½ cups (1 packet) honey-coated banana chips

glaze to taste (see page 19)

Pour the soy milk into the breadmaker bucket, then add the oil and half the flour. Sprinkle with the salt and sugar. Cover with the remaining flour and mound the yeast into the centre. Fit the bucket into the breadmaker and set to the programme recommended in the manual (usually basic white or No 1), adding the banana chips as soon as the machine bleeps. When ready, carefully shake the loaf out of the bucket on to a wire cooling rack and stand the right way up. If liked, brush with the selected glaze. Leave the loaf for at least an hour before cutting and/or removing the paddle if necessary.

WHITE GRAPE AND LEMON LOAF

A firm and well-structured bread, in tune with any fish meal. Or eat it for breakfast sliced and buttered with a topping of marmalade or fragrant flower honey.

300 ml/11 fl oz/1⅜ cups white grape juice

2 tbsp oil

3 tsp finely grated lemon zest

450 g/16 oz/3 cups strong brown (wholemeal) bread flour

1½ tsp salt

1½ tsp caster sugar

1¼ tsp instant or fast-acting dried yeast

glaze to taste
(see page 19)

Pour the grape juice into the breadmaker bucket, then add the oil, lemon zest and half the flour. Sprinkle with the salt and sugar. Cover with the remaining flour and mound the yeast into the centre. Fit the bucket into the breadmaker and set to the programme recommended in the manual (usually wholemeal). When ready, carefully shake the loaf out of the bucket on to a wire cooling rack and stand the right way up. If liked, brush with the selected glaze. Leave the loaf for at least an hour before cutting and/or removing the paddle if necessary.

doughs

DOUGHS

Making doughs couldn't be simpler in a breadmaker as the mixing and kneading processes are taken care of once the breadmaker bucket has been loaded with the selected ingredients. Set the programme to dough, switch on the power and come back an hour or so later to finish off the rolls, loaves or buns by hand. It's a terrific energy saver and with so many people complaining of neck and shoulder problems, the machine takes the strain and does all the hard work, like the heavy-duty kneading that tugs at the muscles. Your final and only involvement is simply shaping the dough according to the recipe, then leaving it to rise before baking in a conventional oven, preheated to the temperature recommended in the recipe.

NOTES

◆ If using a fan oven, the temperature should be lowered by 25°C. You can also place the dough in any position in the oven as the heat circulates evenly throughout the chamber and the top is no hotter than the middle or base.

◆ It may be necessary to leave the dough in the bucket to carry on rising even after the programme has finished, until it reaches almost to the top and/or doubles in size.

◆ As a matter of interest, experts claim the way to tell a first-class dough is if it squeaks on handling. All the machine doughs do!

◆ When leaving doughs to rise, you can do so either in an airing cupboard for speed, in the kitchen or, for a slower rise, in the refrigerator.

◆ To freeze fresh dough, wrap in oiled clingfilm and store for about 5 days. Before using, unwrap, stand on a floured surface and bring back to room temperature before shaping. Allow to rise and bake according to the recipe. Spare cooked breads and rolls may be frozen for up to two or three weeks in plastic bags and reheated in a warm oven or microwave.

MALTED COUNTRY ROLLS

An easy option to start off with, these plain and soft-sided granary-style rolls are as light and spongy as buns and go equally well with sweet and savoury foods.

Makes 12

275 ml/10 fl oz/1¼ cups water plus 2 tbsp

2 tbsp oil, melted butter or margarine

450 g/16 oz/3 cups country grain strong brown flour with malted wheat flakes plus 1 tbsp

2 tsp salt

2 tsp caster sugar

7 g sachet instant or fast-acting dried yeast

extra flour for dusting

Pour the water into the breadmaker bucket, then add the oil or melted butter or margarine and half the flour. Sprinkle with salt and sugar, cover with remaining flour and mound yeast into the centre. Fit the bucket into the breadmaker and set to the dough programme. When ready (see page 134), remove the dough from the bucket and quickly knead on a floured surface. Divide the dough into 12 equal-sized pieces and roll each into a ball, keeping your hands well floured. Transfer to a large greased tray so that the rolls form a square with just a little room between each. Cover with a piece of oiled or buttered greaseproof or baking paper and leave to rise until double in size and the rolls have joined together. Brush with a little water, then dust with flour. Bake for about 25–30 minutes at 220°C/425°F/gas mark 7. Separate into individual rolls and cool on a wire rack. Eat as fresh as possible.

BROWN ROLLS

Prepare and bake exactly as for Malted Country Rolls, but use ½ strong white bread flour and ½ strong brown bread flour and increase the water to 300 ml/11 fl oz/1⅜ cups.

SOFT WHITE BATCH ROLLS

Prepare and bake exactly as for Malted Country Rolls, but omit the extra 2 tbsp water and 1 tbsp flour. Add 2 tbsp skimmed dried milk powder or granules with the salt and sugar.

DINNER ROLLS

An assortment of white rolls for more formal occasions.

275 ml/10 fl oz/1¼ cups water

1 tbsp oil or melted butter or margarine

450 g/16 oz/3 cups strong white bread flour

2 tsp salt

2 tsp caster sugar

7 g sachet instant or fast-acting dried yeast

a little melted butter or margarine, for glazing

Pour the water into the breadmaker bucket, then add the oil or melted butter or margarine and half the flour. Sprinkle with the salt and sugar. Cover with the remaining flour and mound the yeast into the centre. Fit the bucket into the breadmaker and set to the dough programme. When ready (see page 134), remove the dough from the bucket and quickly knead on a floured surface. Divide into the required number of pieces and shape as preferred (see below).

DINNER ROLL VARIATIONS
For flavour changes, add any one of the following dough recipe with the salt:

1 tsp tandoori spice mix

1 tbsp mild, medium or strong curry powder

2 tsp herbes de Provence

1–2 tsp dried basil

3 tsp fennel or caraway seeds

2 tsp sweet paprika

2 tsp dry mustard powder

2 tsp onion or garlic salt *instead* of the plain salt

3 tbsp coarsely chopped salted peanuts, walnuts or toasted almonds

3 tbsp dried onions, dry-fried in a non-stick pan until golden. (Turn often and watch carefully as the onions burn easily.)

RESTAURANT ROLLS
Makes 12

Divide the dough into 12 pieces. Roll the pieces into smooth balls and stand on a greased baking tray. Using kitchen scissors, cut a cross on the top of each, then gently pull up the four points. Cover with oiled baking paper and leave to rise until light and puffy. Do not allow to over-rise or the rolls will lose their shape and definition. Brush with a little lightly beaten egg white and bake at 220°C/425°F/gas mark 7 for about 10–15 minutes until well risen and brown. Cool on a wire rack and eat as fresh as possible.

SPLIT TIN ROLLS
Makes 12

Divide the dough into 12 pieces. Roll the pieces into smooth balls, then shape into ovals. Transfer to a greased baking tray and make a fairly deep lengthwise slit along the length of each with the back of a knife, taking care not to cut through to the base. Cover with greased paper and leave to rise until light and puffy. Do not allow to over-rise or the rolls will lose their shape and definition. Brush with a little lightly beaten egg white and bake at 220°C/425°F/gas mark 7 for about 10–15 minutes until well risen and brown. Cool on a wire rack and eat as fresh as possible.

KNOTS
Makes 12

Divide the dough into 12 pieces. Roll the pieces into smooth balls, then roll each between the hands to make 20 cm/8 in long ropes. Tie into simple and loose knots and transfer to one or two greased baking trays. Cover with oiled baking paper and leave to rise until light and puffy. Do not allow to over-rise or the rolls will lose their shape and definition. Brush with a little lightly beaten egg white and bake at 220°C/425°F/gas mark 7 for about 10–15 minutes until well risen and brown. Cool on a wire rack and eat as fresh as possible.

COILS OR SEASHELLS
Makes 12

Divide the dough into 12 pieces. Roll the pieces between the hands to make 25 cm/10 in long ropes. Transfer to one or two greased baking trays, coiling the ropes as you do so to resemble shells. Cover with oiled baking paper and leave to rise until light and puffy. Do not allow to over-rise or the rolls will lose their shape and definition. Brush with a little lightly beaten egg white and bake at 220°C/425°F/gas mark 7 for about 10–15 minutes until well risen and brown. Cool on a wire rack and eat as fresh as possible.

HAMBURGER BUNS
Makes 10

Divide the dough into 10 pieces and roll out to about 1¼ cm in thick rounds. Transfer to one or two greased trays. Cover with oiled baking paper and leave to rise until light and puffy. Brush with a little lightly beaten egg white or milk and bake at 220°C/425°F/gas mark 7 for about 10–15 minutes until well risen and brown. Cool on a wire rack and eat as fresh as possible.

BAP ROLLS
Makes 9

Prepare and bake exactly as for Hamburger Buns but divide dough into 9 pieces instead of 10. Brush with milk instead of egg, then dust with flour before baking.

ROLL GLAZES
If liked, brush the tops of the rolls with one of the following:

Beaten egg white, egg yolk beaten with a little water, or whole beaten egg
Milk
About 1 tbsp hot water in which 2 tsp caster sugar has been dissolved

ROLL TOPPINGS
If liked, sprinkle the tops of the glazed rolls with one of the following:

Poppy, fennel, caraway, sesame or Indian black mustard seeds (available from Barts or Indian food shops)

CROISSANTS

Croissants made with pure butter are France's traditional breakfast food, served with yet more butter, chunky jam and massive cups of coffee. Eaten warm and freshly baked, they are gastronomic heaven, but they do require more effort to put together than many other rolls and also need refrigerator space for resting.

Makes 6

275 ml/10 fl oz/1¼ cups water less 3 tbsp

25 g/1 oz/⅛ cup melted butter

1 medium egg, beaten

450 g/16 oz/3 cups strong white bread flour

1½ tsp salt

2 tsp caster sugar

7 g sachet instant or fast-acting dried yeast

200 g/7 oz/⅞ cup chilled butter

1 medium beaten egg mixed with 2 tsp water and 2 tsp caster sugar, for brushing

Pour the water, melted butter and egg into the breadmaker bucket, then add half the flour. Sprinkle with salt and sugar, cover with remaining flour and mound the yeast into the centre. Fit the bucket into the breadmaker and set to the dough programme. When ready (see page 134), remove the dough from the bucket and quickly knead on a floured surface. Roll out into a rectangle measuring 46 x 18 cm/18 x 7 in. Wearing a plastic glove, hold and grate the chilled butter directly on to the top two-thirds of the dough, leaving a small border clear all the way round. Fold into three like an envelope – as you would for puff pastry – by bringing the uncovered portion of the dough to the centre and the buttered third over. Press the edges firmly together with a floured rolling pin, then slip the folded dough into a buttered or oiled plastic bag and refrigerate for 45–60 minutes. Remove from the bag and, with the folds to the left and right, lightly roll out the dough into a rectangle as before. Fold into an envelope again, return to the bag and refrigerate a further 45 minutes. Roll out into a thinnish 46 x 18 cm/18 x 7 in rectangle and cut in half lengthwise with a sharp and well floured knife. Cut each strip into six triangles, brush with water and roll up fairly tightly from the base end to the point. Curve into crescents on a large greased baking sheet and cover with a piece of greased paper. Leave to rise at kitchen temperature until puffy. Brush with the egg mixture and bake at 220°C/425°F/gas mark 7 for about 20–25 minutes until golden brown and crusty. Cool on a wire rack and eat as fresh as possible.

BRIOCHE

A glittering star from France, a magnificent giant of a loaf packed with eggs and butter and a touch of sugar. It cuts like a dream and has a smooth and velvety texture, a regal bread of quality and character.

4 medium eggs at kitchen temperature

125 g/4 oz/½ cup butter, melted and cooled

6 tbsp warm (not hot) water

450 g/16 oz/3 cups strong white bread flour

1½ tsp salt

2 tbsp caster sugar

7 g sachet instant or fast-acting dried yeast

a little melted butter, for glazing

Pour the eggs, butter and water into the breadmaker bucket, then add half the flour. Sprinkle with salt and sugar, cover with remaining flour and mound the yeast into the centre. Fit the bucket into the breadmaker and set to the dough programme. When ready (see page 134), remove the dough from the bucket and quickly knead on a floured surface. Cut off an apple-sized piece of dough and reserve. Transfer the larger piece to a fluted and buttered brioche tin with a liquid capacity of 1.5 litres/2½ pts/6½ cups and a top measurement of 20 cm/8 in tapering to 10 cm/4 in. Roll the smaller piece of dough into a ball and place it on top of the larger piece, moistening with water to hold it in place. Gently push the floured handle of a wooden spoon through both pieces of dough. Brush with melted butter, then bake for 10 minutes at 220°C/425°F/gas mark 7. Reduce the temperature to 190°C/375°F/gas mark 5 and continue to bake for a further 25–30 minutes until well risen and golden. Turn out and cool on a wire rack.

FOCCACIA

Italy's renowned flat bread, peasant in character, sublime when eaten oven-fresh and warm, in hunks, with air-dried Italian ham, cold sliced salamis, olives, cheeses, sliced tomatoes sprinkled with basil and garlic or just on its own as a snack with a local red wine. Fruity olive oil added to the dough gives the bread a compelling intensity and fresh herbs contribute their own beloved Mediterranean scent to what has steadily become an established classic. The breadmaker dough was perfection, the bread itself the best of its kind any of us had ever tasted.

275 ml/10 fl oz/1¼ cups water

2 tbsp olive oil, plus extra for drizzling

450 g/16 oz/3 cups 3½ strong white bread flour

1½ tsp salt

2 tsp caster sugar

7 g sachet instant or fast-acting dried yeast

semolina or fine polenta, for dusting

fresh or dried rosemary needles, for sprinkling

Pour the water into the breadmaker bucket, then add the oil and half the flour. Sprinkle with the salt and sugar. Cover with the remaining flour and mound the yeast into the centre. Fit the bucket into the breadmaker and set to the dough programme. When ready (see page 134), remove the dough from the bucket and quickly knead on a floured surface. Shape into a large ball, then press out over the base of a well oiled 30 cm/12 in pizza tin, sprinkled with semolina or fine polenta. Fill in any gaps by stretching out the dough with your fingers – no problem as it is very malleable. Cover with oiled paper and leave to rise until doubled in size; an airing cupboard is useful if you're in a hurry. Dimple the surface quite deeply all over with your fingertips, gently drizzle olive oil into the holes and sprinkle with rosemary. Bake at 190°C/425°F/gas mark 7 for 15–20 minutes or until well-risen and golden-brown. Drizzle with a little extra olive oil and eat warm.

VARIATIONS

◆ Sprinkle with dried basil and coarse sea salt instead of rosemary.

◆ Sprinkle with ready-to-eat and finely chopped sundried tomatoes instead of rosemary.

◆ Stud with black olives, drizzle with oil and sprinkle with grated Parmesan cheese.

CIABATTA

A variation of Foccacia, the bread is named after its appearance – a down-at-heel old slipper or sloppy shoe. A deliciously rustic bread to eat warm and enjoy with anything Italian, especially antipasto and chunky soups.

Makes 2

Prepare as for Foccacia, but add 1 tsp baking powder with the salt and sugar. Divide the dough into two equal pieces and knead each until smooth. Roll out into 25 cm/12 in rounds and dampen the edges with cold water. Fold each into three like an omelette and transfer to one or two well oiled baking trays. Brush with plenty of olive oil, then dust with flour. Bake for 12–13 minutes at 220°C/425°F/gas mark 7 until lightly browned. Turn each loaf over with the help of a spatula. Brush with more oil and dust with more flour and bake for a further 12–13 minutes. Eat while still warm or, if cold, reheat in a medium oven.

PIZZA

No shop-bought pizza can ever match one like this; meltingly succulent and comfortably large with toppings of your own choosing. The quantity makes two pizzas, each enough for four people, but if it's too much for one meal the second can be frozen for up to two weeks.

Makes 2

275 ml/10 fl oz/1¼ cups water

2 tbsp olive oil

450 g/16 oz/3 cups strong white bread flour

2 tsp salt

2 tsp caster sugar

7 g sachet instant or fast-acting dried yeast

tomato purée or passata, for topping

Pour the water into the breadmaker bucket, then add the oil and half the flour. Sprinkle with the salt and sugar. Cover with the remaining flour and mound the yeast into the centre. Fit the bucket into the breadmaker and set to the dough programme. When ready (see page 134), remove the dough from the bucket and quickly knead on a floured surface. Divide the dough in half and roll each piece into a round large enough to fit two 25–30 cm/10–12 in well greased pizza tins, gently pulling and stretching the dough to fit. Pinch up the edges all round to make a lip, then spread with the tomato purée or passata. Cover with oiled paper and refrigerate for 30 minutes (this makes them extra crisp).

After chilling, cover with any of the following: sliced tomatoes; strips of ham and pieces of canned pineapple; red and green pepper rings and pepperoni; flaked canned tuna in oil; sliced mushrooms; streaky bacon; prawns. Finally sprinkle with grated cheese (a mix of ¾ Cheddar and ¼ Parmesan works well) and garnish with black olives and/or canned anchovies. Bake for 20–25 minutes at 220°C/425°F/gas mark 7 when the pizzas should be well risen and the cheese bubbly.

CALZONE
Makes 6

Make the dough as for Pizza (see page 145). Divide into six equal pieces and roll out each one into a 18 cm/7 in round. Brush the edges with water and fill with EITHER chopped skinned tomatoes, grated Mozzarella cheese, 1 tsp dried basil and salt and pepper to taste, OR 150 g/6 oz chopped ham mixed with 200 g/7 oz Ricotta cheese, 1 peeled and crushed garlic clove, and salt and black pepper to taste.

Brush the edges of each with water, fold over to make semi-circles and press the edges firmly together to seal. Transfer to a greased baking tray, cover with oiled paper and refrigerate for 30 minutes. Brush all over with olive oil and bake at 220°C/425°F/gas mark 7 for 12 minutes. Turn over, brush with more oil and continue to bake for a further 12–13 minutes until golden and crusty. Eat while still hot or reheat later in a warm oven.

SUNDRIED TOMATO AND RED PEPPER BREAD

Bread that evokes the flamboyant flavour of Spain and superb with tapas, Spanish snacks which go on all day long with the odd glass of chilled sherry. Over here, have the bread with chilled soups like gazpacho, with olives, with air-dried ham, with Russian salad and egg mayonnaise. It's a tonic.

Makes 2

275 ml/10 fl oz/1¼ cups water

1 tbsp olive oil

2 tbsp Chalice tomato and oregano spread (called tapenade)

450 g/16 oz/3 cups strong white bread flour

1 tsp salt

1 tbsp soft brown sugar

50 g/2 oz/1 cup ready-to-eat sundried tomatoes, scissor-snipped into small pieces

7 g sachet instant or fast-acting dried yeast

extra olive oil for glazing

Pour the water into the breadmaker bucket, then add the oil, tapenade and half the flour. Sprinkle with the salt, sugar and dried tomatoes. Cover with the remaining flour and mound the yeast into the centre. Fit the bucket into the breadmaker and set to the dough programme. When ready (see page 134), remove the dough from the bucket and quickly knead on a floured surface. Shape into two 20 cm/8 in ovals and transfer to a large greased baking tray. Cover with greased paper and leave to rise until light and puffy. Bake for 25–30 minutes at 220°C/425°F/gas mark 7. Cool on a wire rack.

COBBLESTONE BREAD

Prepare as for Sundried Tomato and Red Pepper Bread, but instead of shaping the dough into two ovals, place all the kneaded dough in a well oiled 17.5 cm/7 in round cake tin. Cover with greased paper and leave to rise until the dough domes above the top of the tin. Snip the top all over with kitchen scissors to make a cobblestone effect, brush with water and sprinkle generously with sea salt. Bake for 30–35 minutes at 220°C/425°F/gas mark 7.

LIMPA

An old-timer this, a traditional Swedish classic amid a mind-blowing array of brown breads and crispbreads on offer in every Swedish supermarket and grocer. Basically limpa is a beigy-fawn seeded rye bread with an unusual, slightly sweet flavour and moist texture, excellent with salty foods like pickled and smoked fish. Local variations occur and on a recent visit to the south of Sweden, I spoke with one manufacturer who added lingonberry juice (a cranberry juice taste-alike) to the dough, while other mixes contain beer, vinegar or milk. This version is loosely based on a recipe from the Flour Advisory Bureau in London.

225 g/8 oz/1½ cups strong white bread flour

225 g/8 oz/1½ cups rye flour

150 ml/5 fl oz/⅝ cup water

5 tbsp cranberry juice

5 tbsp milk

2 tsp salt

2 tsp caster sugar

2 tsp caraway seeds

2 tsp fennel seeds

1 tbsp black treacle

1 tbsp golden syrup

1 tbsp oil or melted butter or margarine

7 g sachet instant or fast-acting dried yeast

a little melted butter or margarine, for brushing

Thoroughly mix together the two flours. Pour the water, cranberry juice and milk into the breadmaker bucket, then add half the mixed flour. Sprinkle with the salt, sugar and both seeds, then add the treacle, syrup and oil or butter or margarine. Cover with the remaining flour mix and mound the yeast into the centre. Fit the bucket into the breadmaker and set to the dough programme. When ready (see page 134), remove the dough from the bucket and quickly knead on a floured surface. Shape into one large round loaf and transfer to a greased baking tray. Cover with greased paper and leave to rise until light and puffy. Brush with butter or margarine and bake for 35–40 minutes at 190°C/375°F/gas mark 5. Cool on a wire rack and leave for one day before cutting.

DAKTYLA

Greek-style bread, in harmony with all Greek food. Recipes for it are few and far between so I have based mine on breads previously tried, mostly from Hellenic food shops in south-east England and Greek restaurants. It has an exceptional flavour, curiously sensual, and goes perfectly with full-blown Greek salads and dippy foods like taramasalata, hummus and tzatziki. It's also perfect with Feta cheese made, if possible, with ewe's or goat's milk if you are after the genuine article.

Makes 2

2 tsp sesame seeds

2 tsp black onion seeds

2 tsp anise seeds

275 ml/10 fl oz/1¼ cups water

1 tbsp olive oil

450 g/16 oz/3 cups strong white bread flour

2 tsp salt

2 tsp caster sugar

7 g sachet instant or fast-acting dried yeast

2 tsp caster sugar dissolved in 1 tbsp hot water, for glazing

Combine the seeds in a small dish. Pour the water into the breadmaker bucket, then add the oil and half the flour. Sprinkle with the salt, sugar and 4 tsp of the seed mixture. Cover with the remaining flour and mound the yeast into the centre. Fit the bucket into the breadmaker and set to the dough programme. When ready (see page 134), remove the dough from the bucket and quickly knead on a floured surface. Shape into two 28 x 11 cm/11 x 4½ in rectangles. Transfer to a large greased baking tray and make several deep horizontal slashes on each loaf. Cover with greased paper and leave to rise until light and puffy. Deepen the slashes gently with the back of a knife, brush with the glaze and sprinkle with the remaining seeds. Bake for 20–25 minutes at 220°C/450°F/gas mark 7 until golden and crusty. Cool on a wire rack.

CHELSEA BUNS AND SALLY LUNNS

Chelsea buns were a Court delicacy in the eighteenth century and much favoured by George III and Queen Charlotte. At the same time, Sally Lunns were being eaten in the streets of Bath – supposedly named after the girl who sold them, although another theory says the name came about from Sally's cry of sol et lune, *which translates from the French into sun and moon and aptly describes the appearance of the cakes which were, in effect, yeasted sandwich cakes with a rich filling in the centre. Interestingly, something similar remains a speciality of Dunkirk and comprises two layers of yeasted dough with a rich custardy filling. It's quite glorious.*

Makes 9 Chelsea buns and 1 Sally Lunn

150 ml/5 fl oz/⅝ cup skimmed milk

3 medium eggs, beaten

75 g/3 oz/⅜ cup melted butter or margarine

450 g/16 oz/3 cups strong white bread flour

2 tsp salt

50 g/2 oz/¼ cup caster sugar

7 g sachet instant or fast-acting dried yeast

a little melted butter or margarine, for glazing

EXTRAS FOR CHELSEA BUNS:
25 g/1 oz/⅛ cup butter, melted

225 g/8 oz/1½ cups mixed dried fruit, including peel

125 g/4 oz/½ cup soft brown sugar

icing sugar and hot water, to glaze

EXTRAS FOR SALLY LUNNS:
butter or clotted cream, for filling

icing sugar, for dusting

Pour the milk into the breadmaker bucket, then add the eggs, butter or margarine and half the flour. Sprinkle with the salt and sugar. Cover with the remaining flour and mound the yeast into the centre. Fit the bucket into the breadmaker and set to the dough programme. When ready (see page 134), remove the dough from the bucket and quickly knead on a floured surface. Divide into two equal pieces.

For the buns, roll out one half of the dough to a 30 x 23 cm/12 x 9 in rectangle. Brush with the melted butter, sprinkle with the fruit and sugar, then roll up like a Swiss roll, starting from one of the longer sides. Cut into nine slices with a sharp knife dipped in flour. Place next to each other in rows of three on a greased and lightly floured baking tray, with little gaps between each. Cover with greased paper and leave to rise until the buns join up and are light and puffy. Bake for 20–25 minutes at 200°C/400°F/gas mark 6. Remove from the oven and ice with glacé icing (a mix of icing sugar and water).

For the Sally Lunn, roll the remaining half of the dough into a round large enough to fit a buttered 20 cm/8 in deepish sandwich tin. Cover with greased paper and leave to rise until the dough reaches the top of the tin. Bake as for Chelsea buns, then turn out and cool on a wire rack. Slice horizontally into two layers and fill with a thick spread of either softened butter or clotted cream. Dust the top with sifted icing sugar and serve as fresh as possible with fruit salad or seasonal berries.

BAGELS

The smart roll with the hole in the middle, originally from central Europe and now firmly established in the USA and Britain. The dough used for bagels is basic and simple but there is some effort involved in their preparation prior to baking, which is useful to know before you start, especially if time is short. Bagels freeze well so any leftovers can be stored up to 1 month in a well-secured plastic bag.

Makes 12

275 ml/10 fl oz/1¼ cups water

2 tbsp oil

450 g/16 oz/3 cups strong white bread flour

2 tsp salt

3 tbsp caster sugar

7 g sachet instant or fast-acting dried yeast

sesame or poppy seeds or dried onion flakes, for sprinkling

Pour the water into the breadmaker bucket, then add the oil and half the flour. Sprinkle with the salt and 1 tbsp of the sugar, cover with the remaining flour and mound the yeast into the centre. Fit the bucket into the breadmaker and set to the dough programme. When ready (see page 134), remove the dough from the bucket and quickly knead on a floured surface. Divide into 12 equal pieces and shape each into a smooth ball. Using the handle of a wooden spoon, make a hole in the centre of each. Enlarge the holes by gently pulling the dough outwards so the bagels form rings. Transfer to one or two large greased baking trays, cover with greased paper and leave to rise until doubled in size. In order to set the dough and prevent the bagels from becoming misshapen, place one tray of bagels at a time beneath a hot grill and grill for about 1½ minutes. The distance between the trays and heat source should be about 13 cm/5 in. Carefully turn the bagels over and grill a further minute or so but try to avoid browning. Carefully drop each bagel individually into a large pan of gently simmering water to which the remaining caster sugar has been added. Poach for about 25 seconds, then lift out with a fish slice or slotted spoon and return to the original trays. Sprinkle with the chosen toppings and bake for 15–20 minutes at 200°C/400°F/gas mark 6. Cool on a wire rack, cut in half and, when just cold, sandwich together with fillings to taste. Eat as fresh as possible.

SUGGESTED FILLINGS
◆ cream cheese and smoked salmon
◆ salt beef and mustard
◆ pastrami and horseradish

CARDAMOM COFFEE BREAD

The flavour of Scandinavia is dominated almost exclusively by three spices, ground cardamom first and foremost then saffron and cinnamon, and one herb, dill. This light yeasted cake-cum-bread is a trusted friend throughout the Scandinavian countries and is known in the States as coffee cake, something delicious and comforting to have with a mid-morning drink or as part of a light lunch. The Swedes fill the cake with something like a cinnamon-flavoured butter cream, others leave it plain and it still triumphs beautifully. The ground cardamom is available from Indian food shops.

Makes 2

175 ml/6 fl oz/¾ cup water

2 medium eggs, beaten

75 g/3 oz/⅜ cup butter or margarine, melted

450 g/16 oz/3 cups strong white bread flour

1½ tsp salt

6 tbsp soft brown sugar

2 tbsp dried skimmed milk powder or granules

2 tsp ground cardamom

7 g sachet instant or fast-acting dried yeast

1 medium egg beaten with 1 tbsp water and crushed cube sugar, for topping

Pour the water into the breadmaker bucket, then add the eggs, butter or margarine and half the flour. Sprinkle with the salt, brown sugar, milk powder and cardamom. Cover with the remaining flour and mound the yeast into the centre. Fit the bucket into the breadmaker and set to the dough programme. When ready (see page 134), remove the dough from the bucket and quickly knead on a floured surface. Divide into two equal portions. Cut each portion into three pieces and roll between the hands into 30 cm/12 in long ropes. Plait together in threes. Transfer the two plaits to one or two large greased baking trays and cover with greased paper. Leave to rise until light and puffy, then brush with the egg mixture and sprinkle with the crushed sugar. Bake for 30–40 minutes at 195°C/375°F/gas mark 5. The cakes are ready when they are golden brown and well-risen. Cool on a wire rack and eat warm. As they freeze well, one cake may be frozen in a well secured plastic bag for up to 2 weeks.

HOT CROSS BUNS

The classic British Easter buns with a cross on top, usually of pastry. They're uncomplicated to make, appetisingly spicy, lightly sweet and well-fruited.

Makes 12

225 ml/8 fl oz/1 cup skimmed milk

1 medium egg, beaten

50 g/2 oz/¼ cup butter or margarine, melted

450 g/16 oz/3 cups strong white bread flour

2 tsp salt

5 tbsp caster sugar

3 tsp mixed spice

175 g/6 oz/1½ cup mixed dried fruit, including peel

7 g sachet instant or fast-acting dried yeast

50 g/2 oz shortcrust pastry

golden syrup, for glazing

Pour the milk into the breadmaker bucket, then add the egg, melted butter or margarine and half the flour. Sprinkle with the salt, sugar, spice and mixed fruit. Cover with the remaining flour and mound the yeast into the centre. Fit the bucket into the breadmaker and set to the dough programme. When ready (see page 134), remove the dough from the bucket and quickly knead on a floured surface. Divide into 12 equal pieces and shape each into a smooth ball. Transfer to two greased baking trays and brush lightly with water. Roll out the pastry thinly, cut into narrow strips, dampen with water and use to make crosses on top of each bun. Bake for 20–25 minutes at 220°C/425°F/gas mark 7 until the buns are golden brown. Remove from the oven and brush at once with golden syrup. Cool on a wire rack and eat as fresh as possible.

YORKSHIRE TEACAKES

Generously proportioned cakes and a welcome sight at teatime, They should be split and toasted while still fresh and then spread with butter and eaten straight away, before they have time to cool. Make them for pure nostalgia and recapture countryside tearooms, pretty lace curtains, china crockery and leaf tea with a strainer for pouring.

Makes 6

275 ml/10 fl oz/1¼ cups skimmed milk

2 tbsp melted butter or margarine

450 g/16 oz/3 cups strong white bread flour

2 tsp salt

2 tbsp caster sugar

7 g sachet instant or fast-acting dried yeast

5 tbsp currants

a little extra milk, for brushing

Pour the milk into the breadmaker bucket, then add the butter or margarine and half the flour. Sprinkle with the salt and sugar. Cover with the remaining flour and mound the yeast into the centre. Fit the bucket into the breadmaker and set to the dough programme. When ready (see page 134), remove the dough from the bucket and quickly knead on a floured surface. Knead in the currants. Divide into six equal pieces and roll out each to a 13 cm/5 in round. Transfer to one or two greased baking trays, cover with greased paper and leave to rise until light and puffy. Brush with milk and bake for 20–25 minutes at 200°C/400°F/gas mark 6. Cool on a wire rack.

NAAN BREAD

The essential bread for tandoori chicken and barbecued foods, naan is an Indian flat bread baked traditionally in a tandoor (clay oven). For home use, a grill works perfectly well and the bread looks and tastes remarkably like the real thing. If preferred, strong wholemeal flour may be used.

Makes 6

200 ml/7 fl oz/⅞ cup water

1 medium egg, beaten

2 tbsp groundnut oil

4 tbsp plain yoghurt

450 g/16 oz/3 cups strong white bread flour

2 tsp salt

2 tsp caster sugar

1 tsp baking powder

7 g sachet instant or fast-acting dried yeast

a little melted butter or margarine, for glazing

Pour the water into the breadmaker bucket, then add the egg, oil, yoghurt and half the flour. Sprinkle with the salt, sugar and baking powder. Cover with the remaining flour and mound the yeast into the centre. Fit the bucket into the breadmaker and set to the dough programme. When ready (see page 134), remove the dough from the bucket and quickly knead on a floured surface. Divide into six equal pieces and roll each into an oval measuring 25 x 10 cm/ 10 x 4 in. An exact size is not vital as the bread looks more natural if it's unevenly shaped. Place on a well oiled baking trays and set 10 cm/4 in under a preheated hot grill. Cook for 2–3 minutes until puffy, then carefully turn over and grill for a further 2–3 minutes until the bread is lightly brown. Eat warm.

COILED CHALLAH

The Challah Bread recipe on page 30 explains what the loaf is, and this version is shaped into the traditional Sabbath coil. A large loaf with good keeping qualities, the dough may also be divided into three, each piece rolled into a strip and then plaited together. The poppy seed topping is traditional.

2 medium eggs

water

2 tbsp oil

450 g/16 oz/3 cups strong white bread flour

1½ tsp salt

2 tbsp caster sugar

7 g sachet instant or fast-acting dried yeast

extra beaten egg, for glazing

poppy seeds, for sprinkling

Break the eggs into a measuring cup and make up to 275 ml/10 fl oz/ 1¼ cups with water. Pour into the breadmaker bucket, then add the oil and half the flour. Sprinkle with the salt and sugar, cover with the remaining flour and mound the yeast into the centre. Fit the bucket into the breadmaker and set to the dough programme. When ready (see page 134), remove the dough from the bucket and quickly knead on a floured surface. With floured hands, shape into a 70 cm/28 in long roll. Coil loosely on to a large greased baking tray. Cover with greased paper and leave to rise until doubled in size. Brush with beaten egg, sprinkle with poppy seeds and bake for 30–40 minutes at 190°C/375°F/gas mark 5 until the loaf is brown and crusty. Cool on a wire rack.

CHALLAH PLAIT

Prepare the dough as for Coiled Challah, but divide into three equal pieces and shape each into a 35 cm/ 14 in long rope, tapering the ends so that each rope is thicker in the middle. On a large greased baking tray, loosely but neatly plait the three ropes together, pinching the ends together with fingers dipped in water. Cover with greased paper and leave to rise until doubled in size. Brush with beaten egg, sprinkle with poppy seeds and bake for 30–40 minutes at 190°C/375°F/gas mark 5 until the loaf is brown and crusty. Cool on a wire rack.

CORNISH SAFFRON CAKE

Originally from Cornwall, where saffron production was once an important industry, this looks more like a loaf than a cake and is brilliantly golden-hearted, sweetly scented with saffron and mixed spice and enriched with butter and dried fruit – a momentous revival of times past. It's a super tea-time bread with fresh butter and honey or home-made jam, and may also be eaten at breakfast with cream or cottage cheese and a suggestion of marmalade. It toasts beautifully.

1 sachet Schwarz saffron strands (1 tsp loosely packed or 0.4g)

150 ml/5 fl oz/⅝ cup hot water

2 medium eggs at room temperature, beaten

75 g/3 oz/⅜ cup butter or margarine, melted

450 g/16 oz/3 cups strong white bread flour

1½ tsp salt

6 tbsp caster sugar, plus extra for sprinkling

3 tbsp dried skimmed milk powder or granules

1½ tsp mixed spice

7 g sachet instant or fast-acting dried yeast

175 g/6 oz/1⅛ cups mixed dried fruit, including peel

Soak the saffron in the hot water until the water is completely cold, then pour into the breadmaker bucket. Add the eggs, butter or margarine and half the flour. Sprinkle with the salt, sugar, milk and mixed spice. Cover with the remaining flour and mound the yeast into the centre. Fit the bucket into the breadmaker and set to the dough programme. When ready (see page 134), remove the dough from the bucket and quickly knead on a floured surface. Work in the dried fruit evenly, then shape to fit a 1.5 litre/2½ pt/6½ cup buttered and floured rectangular 900 g/2 lb loaf tin. Cover with buttered paper and leave in a warm place to rise until the dough reaches the top of the tin and domes. Brush gently with cold water and sprinkle with a few teaspoonfuls of sugar. Bake for 30–35 minutes at 190°C/375°F/gas mark 5. Allow to cool in the tin for 10 minutes before turning out on to a cooling rack.

FLOUR-DUSTED SALAMI AND OREGANO BATONS

Rugged and rustic, this off-beat bread is a memorable meal in itself and calls for a forceful red wine to go with it. It smacks of an Italian summer, maybe in and around the Tuscan hills, surrounded by wild flowers and a profusion of aromatic herbs underfoot.

Makes 2

275 ml/10 fl oz/1¼ cups water

3 tbsp fruity olive oil

450 g/16 oz/3 cups soft grain strong white bread flour

2 tsp salt

2 tsp caster sugar

1 tbsp dried oregano

7 g sachet instant or fast-acting dried yeast

150 g/5 oz Italian salami, coarsely chopped

flour, for dusting

Pour the water into the breadmaker bucket, then add the oil and half the flour. Sprinkle with the salt, sugar and oregano, cover with the remaining flour and mound the yeast into the centre. Fit the bucket into the breadmaker and set to the dough programme. When ready (see page 134), remove the dough from the bucket and quickly knead on a floured surface. Work in the salami evenly, then divide the dough into two equal-sized pieces. Shape each into a baton, transfer to one or two oiled and floured baking trays and make six fairly deep diagonal cuts on top of each. Cover with oiled paper and leave to rise in a warm place to rise until doubled in size. Brush with water, then dust with flour. Bake for 30 minutes at 200°C/400°F/gas mark 6. Allow to cool briefly on a cooling rack, then tear off pieces at the cuts. Eat while still warm.

PISSALADIERE

A southern France institution, pissaladière is basically a kind of onion, anchovy and black olive bread and is a distant relative of pizza. It is sold in street markets in great big oblongs, still warm and dripping with oil. I can remember eating it in Nice many years ago and wondering how anything this simple could taste so good.

1 kg/2¼ lb onions

4–6 garlic cloves

5 tbsp olive oil

275 ml/10 fl oz/1¼ cups water

450 g/16 oz/3 cups strong white bread flour

2 tsp coarse sea salt

2 tsp caster sugar

7 g sachet instant or fast-acting dried yeast

100 g/3½ oz jar anchovies in oil

4 medium tomatoes, sliced

100 g/3½ oz pitted black olives

Peel the onions and garlic and slice thinly. Transfer to a large frying pan with 3 tbsp of the olive oil. Cover and fry VERY GENTLY for about 40 minutes until the onions are soft and golden, turning fairly frequently.

Pour the water into the breadmaker bucket, then add the remaining oil and half the flour. Sprinkle with the salt and sugar, cover with the remaining flour and mound the yeast into the centre. Fit the bucket into the breadmaker and set to the dough programme. When ready (see page 134), remove the dough from the bucket and quickly knead on a floured surface. Roll out to a fairly thin rectangle and transfer to a greased and floured 40 x 28 cm/15 x 11 in Swiss roll tin. Gently pull and stretch the dough to fit the tin, then cover with the fried onions and garlic. Arrange the anchovies and tomato slices top, stud with the olive, then trickle over any remaining anchovy oil. Leave uncovered and allow to rise in a warm place for about 20 minutes. Bake for 25 minutes at 225°C/425°F/gas mark 7. Cut into portions and serve while still warm.

CHEESE AND HORSERADISH MUFFINS

Large savoury cup cakes which are soft and tender, warmly flavoured and handsome; a brunch special attraction and fabulous with eggs and bacon.

Makes 12

150 ml/5 fl oz/⅝ cup skimmed milk

4 tbsp water

100 g/3½ oz/⅜ cup butter, melted

1 medium egg, lightly beaten

500 g/17½ oz/3½ cups strong white bread flour

1½ tsp salt

3 tsp caster sugar

2 tsp hot horseradish, coarsely grated (bought ready-prepared in a jar)

100 g/3½ oz /1 cup mature Cheddar cheese, grated

7 g sachet instant or fast-acting dried yeast

beaten egg, for brushing

Pour the milk and water into the breadmaker bucket, then add the butter, egg and half the four. Sprinkle with the salt, sugar, horseradish and three-quarters of the cheese. Cover with the remaining flour and mound the yeast into the centre. Fit the bucket into the breadmaker and set to the dough programme. When ready (see page 134), remove the dough from the bucket and quickly knead on a floured surface. Divide into 12 equal pieces and roll each into a smooth ball. Transfer to a 12-section bun tin lined with large paper cases, North African muffin size. Cover with buttered paper and leave to rise in a warm place until doubled in size. Brush with egg, sprinkle with the remaining cheese and bake for 20 minutes at 200°C/400°F/gas mark 6. Eat while still warm.

faults and reasons

1 Fault:

Bread sinks, leaving a crater or dip in the middle.

Reason:

Bread can do this when it is fed excess yeast. It rises too much, is unable to get the support it needs from the gluten structure and so collapses. Check the amount of yeast in the recipe and make sure next time you use LEVEL teaspoons. Alternatively cut back the yeast by ¼ tsp for every 450 g/16 oz/3 cups of flour or ½ tsp if you're making a bigger loaf.

Also the salt may have been left out or too much sugar was added.

2 Fault:

Texture is open, coarse and crumbly and the top crust looks puffy in pockets.

Reason:

Identical with Fault 1 as far as yeast is concerned. Also there might have been too much liquid, which can be adjusted next time by reducing it by 1 or 2 tbsp.

3 Fault:

Bread smells strongly of yeast/beer.

Reason:

Again possibly too much yeast, but this could also be caused through using stale ingredients and yeast a bit passed its use-by date, or the wrong yeast. This also happens if you are not meticulous about level teaspoon measures. (See section on yeast, page 16.)

4 Fault:

Bread spills over the sides of the bucket and causes a mess in the machine, or sticks to the lid.

Reason:

Too much mixture for the capacity of the bucket. Not enough sugar and salt used or, again, too much yeast. Remember that to some extent it is salt that controls the behaviour of yeast.

5 Fault:

Dough poorly risen.

Reason:

There are several causes for this. The liquid might have been too warm (over 40°C/105°F), which destroyed the action of the yeast. Not enough yeast might have been used in the first place or it was stale and/or the wrong kind. It's possible the water was insufficient, so add an extra tablespoon next time. The ingredients may have been fridge temperature instead of kitchen. Too much sugar might have been added. You may live in a very hard water area with alkaline water, so add 1 tsp of an acid like lemon juice to the water as a counterbalance.

6 Fault:

Crust is too pale or too dark.

Reason:

If too pale, the crust setting on the breadmaker was set too low or there was insufficient sugar added. If too dark, there was too much sugar.

7 Fault:

Baked loaf moist and soggy.

Reason:

The loaf was left in the bucket for too long after baking. It should be turned out on to a wire rack within 5 to 10 minutes to lose moisture-making steam, unless the machine is geared to keep the loaf warm, dry and crisp for up to an hour. Check with your manual. After turning out, it must then be left for at least 30 minutes, preferably an hour, before cutting.

8 Fault:

Bread cuts unevenly into squashy slices and seems tacky, or has been made too wet by the addition of foods like sliced gherkins or olives.

Reason:

Bread was cut too soon after being baked.

9 Fault:

There is a distinct smell of burning.

Reason:

The bread rose too much and fell over the sides and on to the element. Switch off at the power, remove the bucket and tip out the contents. Clean out the machine when it is completely cold and start again with an amended recipe. See Fault 4, page 165.

10 Fault:

Top crust floury.

Reason:

The paddle was put in incorrectly. Check your manual.

11 Fault:

Loaf becomes mildewy despite cool and careful storage.

Reason:

Wet ingredients, like chopped olives, or fresh ingredients such as herbs, were added to the mix. Unless stated otherwise, additions should be dry.

easy conversion charts

FOR ALL BROWN AND WHITE FLOUR

grams	exact metric equivqlent	ounces
25 g	28.35	1 oz
50 g	56.70	2 oz
75 g	85.05	3 oz
100 g	99.75	3½ oz
125 g	113.40	4 oz
150 g	149.10	5¼ oz = 1 cup flour
175 g	170.10	6 oz
200 g	198.45	7 oz
225 g	226.80	8 oz
250 g	255.15	9 oz
275 g	283.50	10 oz
300 g	311.85	11 oz
350 g	340.02	12 oz
375 g	368.55	13 oz
400 g	396.90	14 oz
425 g	425.25	15 oz
450 g	453.06	16 oz = 3 cups flour
475 g	481.95	17 oz
500 g	495.78	17½ oz
525 g	524.13	18½ oz
550 g	552.48	19½ oz
575 g	566.46	20 oz = 3⅞ cups flour

FOR LIQUIDS

ml	exact metric equivalent	fluid oz	cups
25 ml	28.41	1 fl oz	⅛ cup
50 ml	56.82	2 fl oz	¼ cup
75 ml	85.23	3 fl oz	⅜ cup
125 ml	113.64	4 fl oz	½ cup
150 ml	142.05	5 fl oz	⅝ cup
175 ml	170.46	6 fl oz	¾ cup
200 ml	198.87	7 fl oz	⅞ cup
225 ml	227.28	8 fl oz	1 cup
250 ml	255.69	9 fl oz	1⅛ cups
275 ml	284.10	10 fl oz	1¼ cups
300 ml	312.51	11 fl oz	1⅜ cups
350 ml	340.92	12 fl oz	1½ cups
375 ml	369.33	13 fl oz	1⅝ cups
400 ml	397.74	14 fl oz	1¾ cups
425 ml	426.15	15 fl oz	1⅞ cups
450 ml	454.56	16 fl oz	2 cups

SPOONS

1 tbsp = 15 ml   1 tsp = 5 ml

IMPORTANT

◆ Each 8 fl oz plastic cup measure of flour equals approximately 150 g/5¼ oz. Therefore 450 g is taken to be 16 oz or 1 lb flour. Other ingredients, such as sugar or cheese, will have different weights for the cup measure, i.e. ½ cup of white sugar equals about 125 g/4 oz. Therefore, and to prevent too much confusion, I have used spoon measures wherever this has made practical sense.

◆ Use one set of measures only. You can use metric, imperial or cup measures as you prefer, but never a combination.

◆ The smaller loaf, using 450 g/1 lb/3 cups of flour, is about 700 g or 1½ lb baked weight. The larger loaf, using 500 g/17½ oz/3⅞ cups of flour, is about 800 g or 1¾ lb baked weight.

◆ Weight variations will occur, depending on additives. To be on the safe side, check settings for both sizes in your manual to ensure your particular breadmaker has settings for different sizes of loaf. Some do, some don't.

◆ Quantities given in brackets in some of the recipes are for larger size loaves.

stockists and suppliers

BREAD MACHINE MANUFACTURERS

Hinari
Harvard House
14–16 Thames Road
Barking
Essex IG11 0HX
tel: 020 8787 3111

Panasonic
Panasonic House
Willoughby Road
Bracknell
Berkshire RG12 8FP
tel: 01344 862 444

PIFCO (Russell Hobbs)
Failsworth
Manchester M35 0HS
tel: 0161 947 3000

Prima International
4 Elland Park Industrial Estate
Elland Way
Leeds LS11 0EY
tel: 0113 251 1500
www.prima-international.com

Pulse Home Products Ltd (Breville)
Vine Mill
Middleton Road
Royton
Oldham OL2 5LN
tel: 0161 652 1211

BREAD MACHINE RETAILERS

Bread machines are available from electrical shops, department stores, kitchenware shops and some larger supermarkets.

Allders
tel: 0800 528 7000

Argos
tel: 0870 600 3030

Comet
tel: 0845 600 7002

Currys
tel: 0500 304 304

Debenhams
tel: 020 7408 4444

John Lewis Partnership
tel: 020 7629 7711

Harrods
Knightsbridge
London SW1X 7XL
tel: 020 7730 1234

House of Fraser
tel: 020 7963 2000

Jenners
Princes Street
Edinburgh
tel: 0131 225 2442

Miller Brothers
tel: 01302 321 333

Selfridges
40 Oxford Street
London W1A 1AB
tel: 020 7629 1234

Tempo
tel: 0870 543 5363

Scottish Power
tel: 0800 027 3322

FLOUR MANUFACTURERS AND RETAILERS

The following flour mills, bakeries and food halls are worth visiting, Most mills sell flour direct, but it is best to telephone before visiting.

Clarke's
122 Kensington Church Street
Nottinghill Gate
London W8 4BH
tel: 020 7229 2190

Country Market
139–146 Golder's Green Road
London NW11 8HB
tel: 020 8455 3289

Crowdy Mill
Bow Road
Totnes
Devon TQ9 7HU
tel: 01803 732 340

Doves Farm Foods Ltd
Salisbury Road
Hungerford
Berkshire RG17 0RF
tel: 01488 684 880

Harrods Food Hall
Knightsbridge
London SW1X 7XL
tel: 020 7730 1234

Harvey Nichols Food Hall
109–125 Knightsbridge
London SW1X 7RJ
tel: 020 7235 5000

Letheringsett Watermill
Riverside Road
Letheringsett
Norfolk NR25 7YD
tel: 01263 713 153

Neal's Yard Bakery
6 Neal's Yard
London WC2H 9DP
tel: 020 7836 5199

Rushall Mill
Rushall
Pewsey
Wiltshire SN9 6EB
tel: 01980 630 335

Selfridges Food Hall
40 Oxford Street
London W1A 1AB
tel: 020 7629 1234

Shipton Mill Limited
Long Newton
Nr Tetbury
Gloucestershire GL8 8RP
tel: 01666 505 050

The Flour Bag
Burford Street
Lechlade
Gloucestershire GL7 3AP
tel: 01367 252 322

The Old Farmhouse Bakery
Steventon
Nr Abingdon
Oxon OX13 6RP
tel: 01235 831 230

Villandry Foodstore
170 Great Portland Street
London W1N 5TB
tel: 020 7631 3131

West Mill Foods Ltd (Allinson)
10 Dane Street
Bishop's Stortford
Hertfordshire CM23 3XS
tel: 01279 658 473

SCOTLAND

Aberfeldy Water Mill
Mill Street
Aberfeldy
Tayside PH15 2BG
tel: 01887 820 803

Valvona & Crolla
19 Elm Row
Edinburgh EH7 4AA
tel: 0131 556 6066

WALES

The Village Bakery
Melmerby Road
Melberby
Penrith
Cumbria CA10 1HE
tel: 01768 881 515

Derwen Bakehouse
Museum of Welsh Life
St Fagans
Cardiff
Glamorgan CF5 6XB
tel: 01222 573 500

GLUTEN-FREE FLOUR SUPPLIERS

Coeliac Society
PO Box 220
High Wycombe HP11 2HY
tel: 01494 437278
www.coeliac.co.uk

Juvela
SHS International Ltd
100 Wavertree Boulevard
Liverpool L7 9PT
Advice line: 0151 228 1992
www.juvela.co.uk
email: info@juvela.co.uk

index

acknowledgements

Thank you to:

My agent, Sheila Watson, for her tenacity and patience.

Karen Sheppard, representative of Allinson flour, who has backed me all the way with enthusiasm, encouragement and, most importantly, efficiency and humour. Without Karen's belief in the project, and boxes and boxes of Allinson flour and yeast generously donated, I doubt if the book would ever have seen the light of day.

The splendid editorial team at Ebury Press, headed by Denise Bates with Lisa Pendreigh and Ciara Lunn, for taking the book on board and then giving it their own brand of special treatment. The results speak for themselves.

Amanda Howard, my cool and collected editor, who has worked with me on more books then I can even recall now with unwavering perseverance and fortitude, crossing all the ts, dotting all the is and tracking all my mistakes like a hawk. A treasure!

The manufacturers and distributors of bread machines who were kind enough to send machines for trial. They include:

Breville; Hinari; Morphy Richards; Panasonic; Prima; Russell Hobbs; and Team Machine. Also tested were: LG and Cookware.

For the products used in the breads, my appreciation also goes to: Blue Dragon for Asian flavourings and seasonings; Chalice Foods for assorted oils, Mediterranean seasonings and mixes such as tapenade; Schwartz for exotics like saffron plus selected herbs, spices and blends from around the world; Juvela for gluten-free bread mixes, and other manufacturers and distributors who also sent samples for testing; Doves Farm for their selection of speciality flours including spelt and buckwheat.